pay attention:
a river of stones

pay attention:
a river of stones

edited by
Fiona Robyn & Kaspalita

Published by Lulu

pay attention: a river of stones
A Lulu book

Selection, introduction and notes copyright
© 2011 Fiona Robyn & Kaspalita

Copyright of *small stones* rests with original authors.

Published in 2011 by Lulu.com
ISBN: 978-1-4467-9622-1

Book and cover design: Kaspalita
Cover Illustration:
http://beastfromeastdraw.blogspot.com

Further reading:
http://ariverofstones.blogspot.com
http://www.writingourwayhome.com

"Go to the pine if you want to learn about the pine, or to the bamboo if you want to learn about the bamboo. And in doing so, you must leave your subjective preoccupation with yourself… However well phrased your poetry may be, if your feeling is not natural – if the object and yourself are separate – then your poetry is not true poetry but your subjective counterfeit."
~Basho

"The art of finding in poetry is the art of carrying the sacred to the world, the invisible to the human."
~Linda Gregg

"Well, I made you take time to look at what I saw…"
~Georgia O'Keeffe

Preface

The challenge: to notice one thing properly every day during January '11, and to write it down.

The result: more than 350 people across the world paying more attention to what was around them, and writing *small stones*. The birth of a new community of daily writers. A new movement - a river of stones.

This book contains a selection of these engaged moments, written both by experienced poets and complete beginners.

Enjoy the prose pieces, savour every *small stone*, and then turn to the back (p117) and learn how to write your own. January was only the beginning. We'll see you in the river.

Pause and take a breath

In that month of midwinter gloom, cold grey skies and overwork, every single day, I thought: *no, I can't summon the energy to notice something and write it down,* and every single day I thought: *and what's more, I don't want to. What's the point?* And every day I moved through these thoughts and did it, and every day I was enormously glad of such a small thing. Glad because it slowed down time and opened up a space, and something else, however trivial, entered the picture. Glad because a daily practice, as I knew from meditation practice, is a powerfully strengthening, stabilising, calming thing. Glad because every time was a reminder that I could pause and take a breath and look elsewhere for a moment whenever I felt sucked into a cycle of overwhelm and powerlessness, as keeps on happening when there's 'so much to do'. Glad because this daily writing of even a few attentive words was truly, wholly writing, and was slowly, slowly easing me back into the flow of a broader impulse and ability to write. And very glad to know that a lot of others seemed to feel the same.

~Jean Morris, *small stone* writer

snow receding
the head of Buddha
greets the new year

Johannes S. H. Bjerg

*

New Year. The sky is full of fireworks and airplanes.

Rodney Wood

*

winter sun
an old bramble blooms
with frost

Polona Oblak

*

counting the dots
four-and-twenty
robber crows

Stacey Wilson

Hoek:
Here at the edge, waiting for the ship, looking out across the baleful night. The lights of the industrial complex on the other side are white and orange, but only the orange ones are picked up by the overcast sky, glowering intensely. And the water, half river, half sea, the water performs a strange trick with the light, it steals and swallows all the bright yellow tones of the sky, and reflects back a blood orange red. The water moves constantly, rolling and roiling, a twitching throat, and the red painted barriers in front of me are contrasted sharply against the white snow covered quay. The wind whips up the petrochemical flare and the whole sky flickers.

jkdavies

*

the red cherry
at the bottom of the glass
bounces
to the beat
from the dance floor

Mary-Jane Grandinetti

*

...it was a dawn of phosphorescent algae, coming in
from the ocean, drifting overland,

a green sun
hung in icicles.

Brenda Clews

a bird flutters in
this hot night at three am.
new year's day . . .
I'm awakened from a dream,
find a feather on the stairs

Margaret Grace

*

Night in the city, watching its light and its darkness from the belvedere, hearing the voices of those who pass by and feeling the cold on the cheeks.

Ana Catarré Lavad

*

After the Snowstorm
The moon, that Salome, slowly sheds tatters of gauze, finally emerges in all her striking glory.

Ruth Feiertag

*

Even through the tree outside my kitchen window, mist, and the bright lights to drive the dark away, I manage to find the heavy moon.

Isabela J. Oliveira

Clouds float in a rose madder wash as a hawk dives.

Yvonne Quarles

*

in the half-light
my neighbour
rakes her garden
dusk gathering
silently around her

Liam Wilkinson

*

Beneath the barren tree,
Two feathers wave
From bird bones.

Susan Sonnen

*

Dull ochre, the crab apples still cling in spiked maroon hedges.

Rosemary Bradshaw

*

Oh slippery morning.
It's eleven twelve.

Tara Dharma

falling snow
and suddenly we stop
for deer

angie werren

*

In the morning, before the sun, we listen to the coyotes. Greyhound Joey cocks his ears to the wild howling of a language he's never known.

Coyotes—
their pre-dawn yipping
stops us cold.

James Brush

*

Winter Allotment
After the frost, a mulch of plants and mud. I pull out brambles, clear out strangled plastic bags. Stepping on pond-stones, I reach over murky water, cut back ornamental quince.

Annie Clarkson

*

Dunkery Beacon, a crown of heathered hill, winter brown and grazed by matching ponies, wet, and shaggy with yesterday's rain. Beyond the great expanse of Quantox rolling down to sea.

Caroline Brazier

Drifts of snow catch on the sides of pine and hold like lichen.

Jennifer Page

*

Prints:
The sidewalk was shoveled
and the only snow that was left
was in the shape of your boots

Tabetha Smelser

*

bright celery of palo verde
soft silver sage of cypress
layered over cerulean sky

Lyn Hart

*

On pale straw stalks brown bulrushes sway, slowly being feathered by the wind.

Sam Pennington

*

My knife halves the lemon
and summer wafts out.

Lori Ann Bloomfield

blueberries
in December ~
divine

dani harris

*

Cost of living:
A splash of green, a dash of red.
Among all,
My onions are costliest, the vendor said.
Come buy from me, he cries hoarse,
Although you'd have to pay through your nose!

Ambika Suman

*

Blush of buds
in trees
along the ridge,

spring so near
the wind is green.

Tom Montag

•thirty-one•
It is like a bonus, the thirty-first day. Suddenly, no more fog. Blinding sun. Raging blue, and lacy wisps of cloud to prove the Earth hasn't stopped in its tracks. Oh, wow. We are never still.

Lis Harvey

A celebration of the ordinary in the extraordinary

"I love it just because it is a stone, because today and now it appears to me a stone."

~Hermann Hesse

Just a stone. Nothing more. And yet when we really pay attention to a stone, what do we notice?

We feel its unyielding density when we curl our palm around its form.

We see the tiny pock-marks in the stone's skin - hundreds of them, thousands – and feel this texture under our skimming fingertips.

We notice the gradations of colour. Here it has the colour of a seal's skin. Here it looks more like a February sky.

We roll it in our hand, as it cools the centre of our palm. Later we take it from our clenched fist and touch it to our cheek – it has absorbed our heat, and now it is radiating it out.

When we are done, we know it. When we are done, it is our stone. We love it.

overnight
the sedum skeletons
in the street corner garden
burst into mid-winter bloom
sporting fat fluffy heads
of purest white

Kathy Wiederin

*

Snowing slowly
as if light
is flaking off the hidden moon.

Susan Elbe

*

winter
has so much
hattedness

Julie Corbett

*

New moon
No moon, no shadow
One dark pebble
Like a pea under one thousand mattresses…

JulesPaige

Small boats stacked like toys on shelves,
Dry docking while the winter rain holds off.
Nearby the 'Dreampedlar' awaits passengers to set sail.

Laura Kayne

*

Walls of grey sleet advance up the loch. Land and sea blur in the mist. Bedraggled horses nibble the sodden, lifeless grass – January.

Anne Stormont

*

Converging Paths:
Kneeling to pick up a scrap of paper
blown in by yesterday's wind -
cat paw prints, a pile of feathers,
and a calligraphy of lizard tracks
drawn in the sand.

Cynthia Sidrane

*

Proud wrought iron railings.
My mind traces along curves
Cast by its shadow.

Caroline Screen

Gray dawn
through Sunday morning silence
a freight train

Kris Lindbeck

*

Repetitive, bickering jackdaws like metal buttons
clanking inside the washing machine.

Rachel Carter

*

On a winter's morning birds scatter across the sky and
fill the bare trees like fluttering scarves.

Shauna A Busto Gilligan

*

Whitetail deer: Little flags skittering through the woods.

Ray Saunders

*

The tall stump stands rotting, heart hollowed, covered
in vines, epiphytes and moss.
I hear the sharp clear voice of a warbler singing.

sc morgan

The green woodpecker blends seamlessly into our uncultivated grass. Only the flash of red, as it bends its head to dig a long beak in amongst the blades, gives away its existence.

Catherine Walter

*

Davy's Grey:
Davy, how did you know
my perfect sky
was this colour?

Blue Perez

*

Through the front window at 42 rue des Champs Elysées: a dozen yellow tulips lazing over the lip of their vase.

Jeannette Cook

*

My makeup palette smells exactly the same as a set of watercolours I had as a child.

Nora Nadjarian

Sitting at my window
a fire engine red bug
drinks the sherbet of dusk

Uma Gowrishankar

*

seven
blue feathers
pulled
left
one drop of blood

Valerie Sonnenthal

*

cyclone:
Wilma passed through last night
bad-tempered bitch

Christine Stanley

*

parking lot quiet—
everyone watches
a Cooper's hawk with a pigeon
when it's over
nothing but feathers

Carmella Braniger

sleet chatter
on the skylight
night wind keens

Terry Ingram

*

Drifts of snow catch on the sides of pine and hold like lichen.

Jennifer Page

*

The sapling's
papery bark
peels in strips
like the velvet
from a stag's
antlers.

Margo Roby

*

clouds
caught
in a meltwater pool
grass grows through
freely

Peter Hughes

Pressure-washed by gale-driven rain, earth softens. Starlings and rock doves jab the grass. Snowdrop bulbs peep through.

Anne Stormont

*

squirrel tracks have melted through the snow to the bare concrete

Gene Mariani

*

In a sun shower
Sonya waits at the lights.
Spencer shelters
under mummy's tumbrella.

Cameron Semmens

*

Birds startle up in a plume
Like fresh-popped champagne.
The cat,
Like the cork,
Rolls lazy in the hot dust.

Lunar Hine

On the black river,
a pair of great-crested grebe nod
towards the ceremonies of spring.

Kate Noakes

Going on a fast

A month of small stones. Because I've observed Lent and, to a lesser extent, Advent for many years, it's not strange for me to "give things up" or keep to some sort of daily discipline, but that doesn't mean it's easy or natural. Making the observations is pretty easy, and writing something is a good but not foreign challenge. What's hard is *not* going into the other areas my mind often inhabits - the regions of opinions, judgments, arguments, where words can be used not only as pointers but as weapons, or proofs of cleverness and erudition. And partly because of that, I think I've found blogging exhausting sometimes, in the same way that coming up with a good meal and cooking it can be exhausting when one does it day after day, year after year; it doesn't mean you don't like cooking, it just means you've run dry. Writing the "stones" was like going on a fast that was simple, cleansing, and healing rather than a deprivation. I plan to incorporate it much more regularly into my writing life.

~Elizabeth Adams, *small stone* writer

Deep in thought,
my eyes slightly crossed,
I glanced at the sign
and thought it said:

IN CASE OF FIRE
USE SITARS

Matt Blair

*

Just finished washing and detailing my motorcycle. Went back inside to wash up and change my clothes. Came back outside and looked up; there's a bird flying my way. I'm standing next to my bike and the bird is still coming. It's flying right over me now. I look up and splat; the bird shit on my bike. I hate birds.

Hector Mendez

*

The mounted deer head wears a Toledo ball cap at a jaunty angle.

Mark Stratton

He brings out the tattered kids' recipe
"I want to try Watermelon Slushy someday."
"Go ahead. There's watermelon in the freezer."
"You have watermelon in the freezer?!?"
He makes enough for everyone.
None of us like it.

Josephine Faith Gibbs

*

jIlaDtah tlhInganmu'ghom
jIjajchu naghHommeywIJ
Dat

(As I was reading the Klingon dictionary
I understood clearly that my small stones
are everywhere.)

Robert Hale

*

There's nothing like an Alberta Clipper blowing about nine inches of snow through Ohio to remind us that it's winter. Yikes!

Kay Dennison

The flying purple Mini
with loose muffler
severed the evening repose
with explosive
farts

Sue Travers

*

early morning
four hills newly popped
happy moles

Daphne Ashling Purpus

*

Wind walking:
so much wind today blowing fine particles
of granite sand into my face. so much
grit in my teeth, when i open my mouth,
    i don't speak, i sparkle.

Cynthia Sidrane

*

dark morning
dark morning —
Vivaldi pours into
waves of sleep

Stella Pierides

A young man madly in pursuit of sound was milking rather than playing the keyboard and shouting at invisible musical ghosts.

Marcus Speh

*

I am trying to catch thoughts
but they are like water in a net.

Catriona Gunn

*

pale sky
two vultures
wheel upward

slow steady
wingbeats

James Brush

*

Blue police domes / flash silently / a woman sits /
by the roadside / weeping

Peter Wilkin

not the notes
but the clicks & squeaks
      on frets

Mark Holloway

*

From a tiny red bud where the cannula failed to slide neatly into my vein, livid petals have emerged, spreading to cover most of the hand. The centre turned a deep angry blue red, before the dying blood seeped further under the skin, discolouring it in a fascinating and horribly compelling rainbow, changing each day.

Vivienne Tuffnell

*

black raven on white snow, twisting, falling like a beached fish on invisible thread.

Jamie Jensen

*

the full moon's light
catching the sparkle of frost

Katie Godfrey

Above the brightly bundled school children
the confectionary roof of St. Stanislaus:
icicles, filigreed crosses, spatula-smooth snow
on pistachio-colored copper --
it's too cold for our breath to go anywhere
but straight up to heaven.

Elizabeth Adams

*

I press the door to where dementia lurks
life bestows a sweet surprise.
It is a good day

Hildred Finch

*

After so many years
the bedroom radiator
finally fixed
she takes down
the wedding pictures
from the walls.

Jon Summers

*

rain dampens the nap
of a black velvet night

Merlene Pugh

Our *small stone* writers

"My father was recently put into Hospice care and dealing with the imminent loss and pain and joy of his journey has become sweeter for me because I am paying attention. That is no small thing."

~Lisa Haight, *small stone* writer

A mother and daughter team working together on one blog. People who had never see themselves as writers before. People who had never written a blog. A woman still in recovery from leukaemia. Experienced writers who had lost their way. Experienced writers who hadn't. Seekers who were interested in the spiritual dimension of writing *small stones*. Those who joined our community and shared their *small stones* with the world. Those who wrote their *small stones*, secretly, into their notebooks. Writers who had recently lost their brother, their dad, their mum. People who wrote 31 *stones*, more, who are still writing them. People who wrote one. Ordinary people. Extraordinary people, every one.

loading the dishwasher:
remembering
how he likes the teaspoons
in a particular slot
and how he said today
when we sat in the garden
"I like the shapes of the leaves on our trees."

Kirsten Cliff

*

urban birdsong:
a noisy fan belt chirps
as the van clatters down the street.

Nan Pasquarello

*

Eight years old: split lip, warts, lice, red eyes. You can't read; you find it difficult to make friends. Best years of your life?

Laura Wilkinson

*

motorcycle caravan: on the shirt of the oldest rider, my grandmother's name embroidered in pink thread

Melissa Allen

Lumpy women congeal in groups
and loosen the seams
of their tight smiles

Kris Monka

*

San Francisco airport, midnight, after helping my son find his luggage, we headed into an elevator. Inside, I saw a label alongside the button for our destination that read, *"Tunnel to Parking Garage"*. I thought to myself, "Do they provide the pick and shovel or did I need to bring my own sledgehammer?"

James Ross

*

Gerald Cleaver is in my ears
talking about Uncle June
and the Great Migration

I'm making a smaller journey
home from the post office
where I checked for word from you

Jason Crane

still doting
over him
after forty years
his quiet
sigh

Mike Montreuil

*

Click, click of the warming oven. Butter sitting out to soften.

Jessica Kramer

*

31 December
As I walked down the street I felt the unthinking love of your thumb, untangling the knot of bone of my shoulder.
This morning, I understood.

Olivia Sprinkel

*

She holds her compact mirror up with shimmering white nails to check out her reflection. Her boyfriend checks out the other women on the beach. She looks around her mirror at him. He quickly looks back at her and smiles.

Meg Tuite

Soft breeze
the weather vane
does t'ai chi.

Peter Lindsey

*

Morning: I reached for the mug of tea on my bedside table. It was early and all I could taste was hot. In the shower I used the still-almost-full bottle of Apple gel bought in a pound shop last summer. There's a reason it's been relegated to the back of the shelf: it smells of factories rather than orchards, of plastic rather than fruit. It's the colour of an abrasive mouthwash and clashes with the pretend limestone tiles.

Bridget Whelan

*

The last brown leaves of autumn are wrenched from the trees. The angry North wind carves its way across the land.

Gina Elizabeth Deen

*

Small town; small corner grocery.
Hoards of teenagers, milling, chatting, texting
Must be a nest nearby.

Allen Taylor

Speaking French; the words slide off my tongue like a sweet liquid.

Freya Pickard

*

Chocolate powder and dark sugar crystals,
A galaxy hovering on the froth on top of my latte macchiato.
I watch some of the stars going supernova.

Nathalie Boisard-Beudin

*

Poetry Evening:
Three adult poets read
Followed by a teenager.
They read from books.
She reads from an iPad.
I like her poetry better.

Robert Hale

*

so the light can shine.
space between words.

Terri Jane Stewart

Norah Jones sings:
"My toes just touched the water."
Outside, soft rain
on hot concrete:
that sizzling smell.

Helen Patrice

*

Lawrence the goat went to his knees this day, face raised to the heavens, caprine smile, appreciating fully the sun

Mimi Foxmorton

*

Lily-blooming clouds curl in a blue-iris sky, waiting for your confession.

Donna Vorreyer

*

The two year old child carefully picks up each bead he spilt in his sister's room; the blue ones first.

Ruth Stacey

*

A264
Bambi asleep
in the gutter

Martin Cordrey

warm winter day
crows rummage in the branches
of a tree shadow

Polona Oblak

Mindfully watching

I have to tell you, readers, I have loved writing a small stone every day for the last 31 days. It's the most glorious exercise in mindfulness, in pulling yourself into this moment, and if you haven't tried it yet please give it a go, if only for a week. My OCD personality means that I will not miss a day in a project like this. No matter what. And therefore I have been constantly on the lookout, vigilant even, for things to write about. It has come as a surprise to find so much going on out there. And an even greater surprise to realise that all that time I spend daydreaming can in fact be spent watching the world out of the window (and then I get to call it meditation). Some things I have noticed:-

- how the bird feeder is in constant use, and squirrels particularly like to eat the fat balls.
- the monkey puzzle tree outside Mayflower flats that has been there since I was a child.
- the way cats sleep with one paw over their noses when it's cold.
- the way my legs have to move to ride my bike.
- the sound of birdsong.
- the number of times people look straight through me. I wonder how many times a day I do that?

I'd like to think I will carry on mindfully watching, carry on writing stones.

~Rachel Hawes, *small stone* writer

in the plum-colored sky
twirling with the city lights
and smoggy contrails--
wolf moon

Kathy Uyen Nguyen

*

Day dies in the arms of night.

masterymistery

*

Alone all day, I draw solitude around me like a cashmere cardigan.

Jenny Maltby

*

Rain falls from blue sky
a chill breeze lifts the leaves
the door is open
but I cannot join the crowd.

Suzie Grogan

*

rain-soaked lawn. wet maple leaves hitch a ride on the soles of my shoes.

Cara Holman

An empty muffin case lies flat and folded in the road like a fan, abandoned mid-dance.

Peggy Riley

*

Running:
Like the bud of a stump
which was meant to be wing,
the fat glutted border between arse
and thigh flaps and shudders
with every step. Not keeping time with my heart.

Mairi Sharratt

*

Cold wind blowing across the meadow in the early morning, as sun tries to open its eye to the world.

Nalini Harvey

*

Listening
to the prayers of snow

In the distance, wind
in a clay bell.

Wendy Sarno

Audible sounds of
dogs breathing and
furnace kicking on

compete with
whistling wind and
cracking branches

as gleeful children
enjoy an unexpected
school holiday.

Judy Shepps Battle

*

Beans bubbling away in the saucepan;
Apple, mustard, molasses, chilli, garlic, onion,
Winter curls slowly upstairs.

Adrian Thompson

*

At the precipice
bearing peace,
a cardinal
sentinel;
love.

Laurie Kolp

Leaden on the swan plant where stained glass should be;
dying monarch.

Rachel J Fenton

*

After each frost the winter jasmine
puts out new candles of yellow flower.

Elizabeth Rimmer

*

a viola playing the scent of a violet

Olivia Dresher

*

Barely freezing
Patterned ice
Untouchably delicate
Forms the pond's new skin.

Caroline Screen

*

Arctic Wonder:
A blizzard of snow leaves behind
Dr. Zhivago's troika. Three horses
rush past and wink at me.

Clarissa Jakobsons

at the wake
her good china
still mint

Jill Stanley

*

no-one to blame
a shutter bangs in the night

Lynne Rees

*

At the damp mossy bases
of sunlit trees,
hellebores and snowdrops face the ground.
In the branches above,
the birds sing.

Sara Kirkpatrick

*

cold clear sky
brightly colored pansies
facing toward spring

Daphne Ashling Purpus

renegade reds dot
a leaf brown landscape—
a pack of newports shouts
viridian blue

Robin Turner

Everywhere is holy

Oliva Sprinkel wrote that this project led her to reflect on darshan. Darshan is a Sanskrit word that means 'to see'. In the Dharmic religions, one might go to a teacher for darshan; to be seen by the teacher as much as to see him or her. In this use of the word there is often a sense that what one is seen by is the divine, or the part of the teacher that is enlightened, and that through this act of seeing and being seen the devotee is transformed.

One might go to a holy place to receive darshan, as much as to a teacher. I believe that all places are holy, that really seeing and really being seen has the power to awaken, to soften the edges of our hard selves and let a little reality in.

Don't let all this talk of divinity scare you off. I use it because I don't have a better word to hand, although I can't really quite grasp what it means. You know it if you see it, or if you are seen by it.

"...the focus is upon discerning the truth of the other and achieving spiritual maturity. One achieves liberation for oneself by releasing others from the attachment generated by one's own deluded and stereotypical perception of them. The self-construct is the mirror image of these false views of others. To see the truth of the other is to release them and thereby, incidentally, to release oneself from one's self-construct."

~Dharmavidya David Brazier

Halving cherries,
I pry the stones
from their black hearts,
blood pooling
beneath
my fingernails

Elizabeth Adams

*

Dimpled, flecked with gold,
the yellow pear's fragrant skin
barely holds its juice.

Jean Morris

*

frosty lemon drop
cracking like ice
in my mouth

Kirsten Nørgaard

*

wild plum trees tower over
the spacious hibernacle
where a june beetle sleeps

Jade Zirino

My compost is fragrant
with the smell of rosemary prunings
and bruised plums.

Catherine Fitchett

*

Oh
An egg!
Glancing into a bowl on the windowsill
A tiny little pale blue egg
All spotted and flecked with brown
With moss stuck to its side
Picked up in the garden last summer
And forgotten about

Claire Arnold-Baker

*

Vegicide: Massacring beetroot in the kitchen, magenta blood drips from my hands. Out damn spot, out I say…

Mel Morris-Jones

*

sweeping
the sun bright floor
dust
illuminated

Richard Cody

after
the cleaning lady goes
my daughter
runs to tell me
we can make a mess

Christina Nguyen

*

I throw fruit instead of passing it nicely because I like the clappy-slappy noise when you catch it.

Martha Williams

*

Its goldenness brimmed over the edge of the crisp skin leaving a pool in the creamy flesh of the perfect potato and puddling on to the porcelain white of the warm bowl.

Jan Friend

*

Sweet onions of Figueres
Fall in violet arcs
On the chopping board

Kate Wilson

winter cold
fishing
for lemon pips

Mat Cross

*

sawing at the rock-hard crust of sourdough, I am the coroner slicing into the skullcap of a prone corpse

Kat Mortensen

*

"Don't you just love it? I bought it!"

Michael Stang

*

M&S Sale:
A row of grey-haired gentlemen sit
Patiently
As their wives scrummage around for bargains

Claire Arnold-Baker

Maple leaves
pressed into
the pavement
by the rain
the pattern
set by ice.

Margo Roby

*

My grandmother's tablecloth
They say old lace is whitened
when washed and hung overnight
outside in heavy frost.
Last night would have been perfect.

Sandra Davies

*

Peel rolls with ginger in the marmalade boil.

Jan Friend

*

Smooth red potatoes, like small bald heads that must be scalped for dinner.

Anne Jeffery

The hedges wear a cloak of finches
holding their frostbitten tongues,
too cold even to sing.

Joseph Harker

*

yunnan pines freeze in tai chi poses

Sidney Bending

*

Bits of broken tree branches
scuttle in the streets like crabs.

One pinches the roof edge
of an Albany brownstone,

hangs on for her life.

Carolee Sherwood

*

Dogs barking rattle the tin shed. A striking green field catches the corner of my eye. A photogenic light. Refocus. Refocus.

Andy Harrod

Above the bleak calligraphy
of trees
on snow's white page
the impossible gentleness
of winter sky

Kris Lindbeck

*

from around the manhole cover
steam rises in pulses
as though beneath the sidewalk
a dragon sleeps...

A.C. Missias

*

My white Go-Go boots still fit so I wore them as I sipped on an old bottle of Red Mountain wine and danced to forty Beatle songs in front of a mirror that revealed my true age.

Stevie Strang

*

Age Gap:
Reading my article, you ask,
'What does LGBT mean?'

Gareth Trew

How evening comes: like a grey tabby slipping
underneath a row of parked cars.

Jeannette Cook

*

glistening shards of glass
mosaic of crumpled foil
chaotic veins of silk

Sheree Mack

*

A little night music -
the shiver of the beads
round your neck

Heike Stehr

*

His blue shirt pocket
Where my ear rests in the dark
Just the sound of air.

Jamey Spain

*

talk of welding, gypsies and the time he swallowed a
matchstick

Joanne E. Miller

hear the heat
cracking the house's joints
feel it
reaching through your walls
gripping you
so softly

Jennie Fraine

*

As if in prayer.
Men on their knees.
New carpet for the crazy golf.

Annie Kerr

*

Sunday recital
the bend of the diva's knees
before the high notes

Jill Stanley

*

108:
thumb
rosary bead
forefinger

Kuvalaya Abel

Listening to Jenny is bonfires and bread. Coaxing crops from the shit that happens.

Sarah Tanburn

A place to lay my weary grief

The River of Stones project has been, for me, a place to lay my weary grief. Every day I've had to stop, take a few minutes and think of my baby brother (an adult but always baby brother to me). He died the week before Christmas and while I already knew I would take part in a river of stones, I had no notion of theme or direction. After his death, I wanted a way to memorialize him and the river seemed a natural fit. Maybe it had something to do with how much he loved nature - maybe it was because I had just relinquished his ashes to a creek that I knew would shortly be joining a river and ferrying him to the ocean, maybe it just felt right - I don't know for sure. What I do know is that the pause in my day that has had me remembering him so that I could write a line or two has been a most remarkable experience. Right from the get-go I decided to pair the lines with small pictures that seemed to work, and that also has been helpful as part of my grieving process. On the one hand, I almost hate to see the end of the month approaching, but on the other am glad to let this go and get going in a bit of a new direction; writing my own way home [our online community] seems just about perfect.

~S. E. Ingram, *small stone* writer

In Memory of WJH

last night I dreamt you
    alive; we were sitting here
        talking as if we had never
            not talked, and things were
                right between us ...
                    when I awoke, my pillow was damp

S.E.Ingraham

*

Woke early, smells of cotton and softener in the duvet. Dark, pitch dark, no sounds, save soft breaths. Remembered last night's conversations. Smiled in the dark.

Julia Chapman

*

Winter Here:
There's sunshine, for the first time in days, and through the window, Meyer lemons, fully ripe; lemon verbena, gone wild with the rain.

Amy Radbill

January morning, a leaden sky.
The lake, a pewter plate.
Staring out the window,
I think, metal and mettle.
I think iron.

Susan Elbe

*

Bill Godfrey:
Camomile tea in a coffee cup.
He asks me, "Raven,
What is time doing to us?"

Raven Garland

*

last word / your hearse slowed in heavy rain

Alistair Cook

*

bare branches
trembling
loneliness in trees

Anjum Wasim Dar

rain   those nameless waters

Johannes S. H. Bjerg

*

joy is circular -
the dog, dumb with it, runs around me
my boys chase each other in a perfect O
at the top of the staircase
everything is white;
a lily unfolding

Ruth Stacey

*

Monday 3 January
Sounds linger under leaden skies. Car tires crunch on gravel, gulls caw, the thump of boots as I walk. And then, despite the stillness, the whoosh and kerrrrrr of waves on a pebble beach.

Claire Marriott

*

my mother's silver bracelets ring quietly in my every gesture

Anna Ekielska

She sits, folded over her pain.

Lizzie Carver

*

Is it wrong to say I wish you the worst?

Courtney Stuker

*

Three goldfish locked in icy synchronicity hang in a dark corner of the pond. Their mouths break the surface water, emitting bubbles that burst in the cold air. A blackbird pecking at the moss on the stone edge above, spots them, then flies away.

Diane Becker

*

an old man walking
braced on a frail wooden cane
through the musty leaves

Laura Lawless

*

baggy trousers
tattered hems
trail in
the dust

Barbara Boethling

winter limbs- she learns her bones by pain

Dana-Maria Onica

*

Dusk:
Driving south in the borderlands of the day
ice moon in the east, sun dance in the west

Avril Joy

*

The still silence
of the Downs
is only broken by
my footfall

Douglas Robertson

*

time out of myself...
snowdrops

Paul Smith

*

The fig tree tosses
its leaves to the floor in play.
My broom plays with them.

Guy A. Duperreault

rainforest
the voices of birds
in ferns
unrolling the sound
of a night-time shower

Jane Reichhold

*

the asparagus fern
suddenly shoots green sprigs
in every direction
one of them sure to hit Spring

Kathy Wiederin

*

A Treatment:
Rain drums on the hut roof, while I lie half-dressed on a heated blanket. Her music is the quiet zheng zheng of a guzheng. She holds a moxa stick near my skin, hovering close until I say hot hot.

Annie Clarkson

*

Early morning sun bleached the tall yellow grass white, while the trees cast elongated purple shadows.

Jacqueline McAbery

Pure honey on my breakfast table, the honeycomb still visible, the dark triumphant golden of the hexagonal walls, the structure that seems to breathe, to concertina, something that you could walk through. I get the taste of luscious, luxuriant gold and its brown undertow, a hint of delicious sin.

Alison Wells

*

The child at the concert
lifts up her arms and plays
a violin made of air.
Her expression is very serious.

Rosemary Nissen-Wade

*

Clean:
the way my son tilted his dinner plate
to lick every drop of saucy
pasta—certainly less common than
a cat scrupulously going at it
from all angles,
skinny leg raised
in mid-air

Irene Toh

You wake up hot and crying
and ask me to tell you a story with a daddy in it.

Laura Rachel Ellen Selway

*

too old for lullabies
i open the small window
& let the rainsound in

Mark Holloway

Where the river meets the sea

"This first week back at work after the long Christmas holiday has been pretty relentless and tiring. Several times I've had the thought that I absolutely don't have the time or mental space or energy to stop and notice something outside my driven daily preoccupations, to compose even this tiny 'small stone' of words. But I keep finding that it doesn't eat up time or mental space; on the contrary, time stops and new space is created".

~Jean Morris, *small stone* writer

To label *small stones* on Twitter, we chose the identifier 'aros', standing for 'a river of stones'.

Kirsten told us that in Danish, this word means 'estuary'. An estuary is the place where the river meets the sea. This book is one of the places where our river of stones meets the world.

Matt told us that 'aros' is the Welsh work for 'wait', or 'stay'. We need to be patient when we are looking for *small stones*. We need to be able to make ourselves still. If we are quiet, *small stones* will show themselves to us. They will create a new space for us.

mud puddles of cinnamon and sugar
a stray gold hair
jazz in the old room

Marianne Disney

*

another morning -

strands of hair
in the washbasin

Cheong Lee San

*

the capital:
woke today and hated capital letters
bullies towering above the others,
thinking they are so special

i abandon capital letters today

Ann Rapstoff

*

The wooden kitchen counter is dry
she has conserved her oil
in five jagged flakes that sparkle at me.

Sonia Jarema

I savour the aroma
of the first coffee of the morning.
It warms me as I watch
the snow falling.

Elizabeth Leaper

*

Anger bursts through the door; six foot four, and two foot three.

Deborah Rickard

*

The storm's coming when the chickens spread out,
searching for breached worms,
then gather tight between the wind and fence.
Checking the scratched earth,
the squirrels scurry with one eye upward.

Jason Riedy

*

The snow whips around Old Lugh's bark with a force that would make a lesser tree crack. But there he stands, greeting me each new day, never complaining, even allowing the winter squirrels to play in his wild, old man hair.

Mimi Foxmorton

Copper-dark carpet
where you fell, before leaving:
cold bed where you slept.

Steve Isaak

*

Through the latticework of leaf and branch, light gets entangled.

Karen Faith Villaprudente

*

Children in the Alder Woods:
Two of the children running light like deer through alder woods, then negotiating the dark green undergrowth, their voices the only clue. I pull back out of their world so they can find their own adventures.

Alison Wells

*

Thursday 2 pm
this serendipitous, circular joy
of having the Jacuzzi
in the swimming hall
all for herself

Dorothee Lang

Afternoon tea:
Hot crumpets on cold plates leave circles of condensation.
A million tiny bubbles reflect the candlelight.

Mavis Gulliver

*

i breathe in all your little boy sweetness

a cherished bouquet
all heat and syrup and soap

as you reach down from the high bunk to
hug me goodnight

your little hand
fitting like the pit of a plum
within mine

Lisa Haight Stott

*

Your belly is flat. Disappointment looms between us,
dark as a bruise, silent as a child never born.

Martha Williams

I had the feeling I knew the man serving me in the shop,
until I realised
he had the face of a friend, long dead.

Ged Duncan

*

Park Bench:
They huddled together
Like rain drenched birds

Manchester Barry Price

*

freezing cold
against my chest
his sweater zip

Kirsten Nørgaard

*

Little glass droplets strung on a necklace -
All my favourite colours captured in one place.

Jen Smith

I love the mischievous snowflakes
gathering on your eyebrows:
frozen fat-bodied faeries
that tumble
from your surprise.

Joseph Harker

*

I drink aromatic Turkish coffee
from his warm cotton shirt.

Uma Gowrishankar

*

Curled up on the couch
Comfy in his winter coat
My dog sighs for me.

Anne-Marie Flynn

*

thin shadows of reeds
reflect on water mirroring sky but
a discarded can of Tennants squats in my poetic vision

Tammy Hanna

ring around the moon
I help my mother cross
the icy pavement

Johannes S. H. Bjerg

*

in deep snow
tiny dog in the same tracks
she forged before

Terry Ingram

*

invisible:
he staggers through the busy shopping streets wrapped in
a surprisingly white duvet

Kuvalaya Abel

*

Shavings / beneath a lathe / pine-scented curls / of
heartwood / aesthetic casualties

Peter Wilkin

*

aching fingers
a small poem
will do for today

Aubrie Cox

The syringe that pushed Doxorubicin into Gary's arm.
Nicknamed the 'Red Devil' for its colour and its side
                                            effects,
an artificial brightness that flooded
my husband's veins and tissues.

Kathryn Taiaroa

*

One tiny shell from Niihau, one polaroid from Eklutna Glacier, one bit of sand from the stairs of the temple of Hatshepsut, a piece of sheep's wool from the hills near Clew Bay, all wrapped in a silk scarf from Istanbul and kept in my grandmother's wooden Bible box.

Sandra de Helen

*

during dinner
a tealight draws a thin line
between conversations

Mat Cross

I ran
climbing stairs
two steps at once
toward the west window
but the sun had already set

I miss it so much!

Dana-Maria Onica

Glimpses of hope

I know that of what I've written so far, most are not actually small stones. Like I said at the beginning, maybe it's enough to write something every day, but I'm not even managing that. Have I failed already then? I don't think so. I am looking more closely and I am thinking more clearly, whether I write it down or not. So, I'm not going to beat myself up but be grateful for the space to reflect on such things. I've been in a pretty negative place lately and that has already changed. I'm feeling grateful for all sorts of things and a joy that has long been absent has reappeared. There are glimpses of hope and so I press on, trying to be more disciplined in my daily writing and reflecting on its value. Perhaps other things have changed that might account for this change of heart, I don't know, but it seems to me that small stones are building new foundations.

~Beth Williamson, *small stone* writer

winter sun
the horse chestnut buds
begin to sweat

Polona Oblak

*

longing for eucalyptus in a room steam-full of pumpkin spice

Sami Knowles

*

first hint of spring:
delicate yellow stars unbramble the fence
their petals balance raindrops

Sarah James

*

Watery sun almost shining through clouds,
Trying to paint treetops with brushstrokes of gold.

Rachel Hawes

*

Paper-thin mushrooms--
like old carefully-sorted love notes --
line an ancient dead tree trunk.

Matt Blair

Rook:
Dalek greeting
Loudly follows me
As I walk to the shops.

Liz Allmark

*

7:20
Only three cars on the whole floor.
I get out, click the button. The beep echoes.
I walk to the trolleys in the semi-dark, trying to ignore
the smell, or at least to pretend I don't recognise it.

Miriam Drori

*

thin shadows of reeds
reflect on water mirroring sky but
a discarded can of Tennants squats in my poetic vision

Tammy Hanna

*

stone hard
as the blank page's
obduracy

Robin Chapman

an explosion of small birds and quail
dark wings sweep the snowy sky

Hildred Finch

*

Page 357, top right corner, squashed fly, one wing.

Joanne E. Miller

*

Exalt the one,
unfairly belittle the rest.
Each moment a beach stone,
"Pick me! Pick me!"

Spongebelly

*

The waves roll in lazily; their whitecaps barely able to touch the shore.

Madeline Sharples

*

Sub-zero temperatures have caused multiple splits in our hose pipe. Washing the car was cold, wet and spiteful.

Elaine Phipps

Northern winds are bending branches
and the birds seek sheltered places
in shaggy evergreen hedges and dry buildings.
It's a cold day in the central valley of California.

Ralph W. Bonds

*

through cold, heavy drizzle
a sharp scent of wood smoke in the car:
the aroma brings warmth

Katilou Curry

*

gingerbread cookies
cut out by tender hands
the horses are cold

Cindy Rinne

*

Morning's blush
reflected on the snow

Michelle Hed

Waiting for a romantic evening spin
Two kookaburras on a clothes line

Gemma Wiseman

*

On our walk back from the rice field, Arnaud picks a fruit I've never eaten before. It's called a "zamborizany" in Malagasy (*Syzygium jambos*), and is about the size of a cherry, pale yellow, and crunchy like a fuji apple. It tastes like roses.

Audrey McCombs

*

afternoon commute
a stream of red taillights
stretches into the distance

Peter Mallett

*

Under the cover of darkness
A lone dog's bark echoes across the fences
Waiting but without reply

Jane Phillips

the cold of the grave claws at my boots

Elaine F.

*

frozen canal
the squall of rooks in the trees
dark cathedrals of noise

Mark Sargeant

*

Drifting through dry leaves,
the fall breeze spreads the fragrance
of the dying year.

Jennifer Jenson

*

Listening to the scritch of plows scraping the road.
A thin snow slanting down.
Everything almost. And fragile.

Susan Elbe

A special kind of reaching out

For most of our lives, we see the world through the thick veil of our small selves: I like peonies, I don't like big dogs, I don't care about nuclear physics. We continually warp our surroundings to suit us, looking for affirmation of those things we already believe, and subconsciously screening out anything that challenges us or makes us feel uncomfortable.

The practice of noticing *small stones* breaks through our habituated responses to the world. It encourages us to really pay attention that big dog, or to listen to that fact about quarks. Over time, it helps us to redefine our likes and dislikes, so we can have a more direct encounter with the other.

"…even on a material level, the other is a great mystery. When we struggle to relate to it, we fall back into personalised approximations. Keeping our sense of wonder and our willingness to encounter the other requires a special kind of reaching out."

~Prasada Caroline Brazier

Aware that January is coming to a close, we walk in the snow
you, focusing on rabbit smells
and I reflecting on what it means to
be here.

Ramona Felse

*

unopened tulips
like a bouquet of mauve
barnacles

Sidney Bending

*

In the snow, a small tree of robins. They scatter evenly
over bare branches,
bobbing fat on the ends like strange Christmas
ornaments, bright, and
feathered, and blinking.

Jessica Kramer

*

The morning birdsong filters through the curtain of rain.

DJ Kirkby

somewhere outside
a dog
sounds like
a child's squeaky toy

Kylie Dinning

*

overcast morning
a decorator
carrying a tin of sky blue paint

Mat Cross

*

The colorless day did nothing to dampen the song of the birds.

Teri H. Hoover

*

green council bags
stretched tautly around their lumpy innards

Kathleen Powell

Commuter
man in
black pea coat—
long strides—
You are a
boy, only
just grown.

Elizabeth G. Howard

*

The wind whips through the lime,
stripped bare for winter, and the tree shivers.
A trio of blue tits flit from one branch to another.

Beth Williamson

*

On its way
To the sea
The stream
Attempts to get
Airborn again

Ainsley Allmark

In the creek,
ice the color

of what trees
dream.

Tom Montag

*

Cemetery:
The scent of flowers, fresh and decayed, drifts sweetly on a breeze as plastic wrappings crinkle; breaking still silence.

Susan May James

*

paint peeling
from the garden wall -
faded roses

Juliet Wilson

*

slender moon
suspended
between power lines

Jade Leone Blackwater

Mizzle falls on the steep green/gray slope where
teenagers sledged only four days ago.

Carol Ritson

*

who scratches at my
midnight door? my rain-soaked cat,
suddenly humble!

Andrew Dugas

*

A tangle of shiny loose wire
Dangles from the fence post
Like a child's scribble picture

Josephine Faith Gibbs

*

Snack:
tossed from the window,
        stale sugar cookies sink
in fresh blankets of snow.

           the birds won't see them till spring.

Christina Rodriguez

A pot of turbid yoghurt.
That is how the sky is today.

Uma Gowrishankar

*

The wind pummels rain and wraps around itself.

Kirsty Stanley

*

my rich neighbor —
late at night
he slowly
peels
an orange

Melissa Allen

*

Whispering in the library of the early morning. Birds chirping as they exchange their neighbourhood gossip. The 5 o'clock traffic chorus on the bypass. Seeds of a story germinating in my imagination.

Maggie Baldry

*

Opening a second-hand book: the sweetness of pipe tobacco, a closed door, silence.

Vanessa Gebbie

Beatrix is allowed to wear her party shoes to school. When teachers and children 'Ooh' and 'Aah' she closes her eyes so no-one can see her smile.

Claire King

*

natural cathedrals the size of my pinkie, caddisfly cases...
glistening wet mosaics of rust, orange, earth, saffron pebbles, slickly fastened into slender-stiff sleeping bags

Sarah Endo

*

Clear mountain stream
Striking hard rock,
Coarse-grained beds
Collecting pools of stillness

Katherine Murray

*

A taxi pulls up
In the African Savannah.
Is taken over by nature.

Tawfeeq Elahi Samad

catching a snippet
of the news
  talk of a patented
  Russian hovercraft

on the next channel
Cherokee holy lands—
  I see how life
could begin
  in those mountains

Aubrie Cox

...slow down

In today's society, we are bombarded with ringing, beeping, texting and instant messaging. We seek immediate gratification through Facebook, Twitter and other social networks. If we need to reach someone, we can usually contact that person right away. I find all my peace and serenity diminishing the further I get caught up in this whirlwind of technology mumbo jumbo. That is why I loved participating in A River of Stones during the month of January; it forced me to slow down and take note of life's simple pleasures. Writing small observations daily was like a spiritual experience for me. I felt happy, joyous and free. I looked forward to my daily meditation. As a result, I feel awakened and alive; and I am truly thankful.

~Laurie Kolp, *small stone* writer

*
the
naked
tree stands
still at midday
its branches aching
for the whisper of
the
wind
Sher Mattison

*

The rain raps incessantly against the carriage windows. Dark descends gloomily over London. Young commuters stare into their smart phones connected to everyone but their fellow passengers.

Peter Domican

*

Several small gray birds
forage under the rose bushes.
A male Cardinal
punctuates their conversation
with his bright red body.

Jessica Plante

Wind chimes jingling a jig
in February's fierce winds.
Birds are dancing
on the lawn.

Steve Wilkinson

*

long afternoon shadows
have passed into darkness,
the call of a cicada
creeps down the garden steps

Lonnard Dean Watkins

*

hackberry hacked clean—
its stump a startled heart,
pale as death now, perfect,
in a hillside sea of green

Robin Turner

*

beneath the soil
mycelium weaves its strands
invisible
feasting on the past
until it mushrooms to the surface

James Newton

In the wood
Lichen covered trees
like hairy old men
who have forgotten to shave

Mavis Gulliver

*

The honey fungus clings to the Ash Tree devouring its soul.

Ann Perin

*

praise for overcast
skies! greys, sweet eye-balm
slathering quiet

Jade Leone Blackwater

*

Hiss of simmering water on the log-stove range. Occasional bird-song from the lime-tree heights beside the cold river.

Nadia Stevenson

Thick with frost, the lawn appears to have grown white fur.

Linda Hofke

*

Night Rivers:
Rain tickles the roof
softens the snow
and traces rivers of silver
down my road

Susanna Holstein

*

My early memories of Hungary
are buses and armpits,
and playing at the lake,
and the huge, newspaper wrapped, whole fried fish
we ate with our fingers.

Barb Black

*

A whimstone ponders,
basking like a shore held seal
thinking tidal thoughts.

Keith Wallis

A pale full moon shines in the backyard
A thin veil of fog forms hangs over streets and alley cats
A drop in the mercury, unpredicted by the 11pm news
A sheet of ice forms, sealing tight my truck's doors

Kevin Peterson

The moon was a French polished fingernail against the dawning sky.

Anne Jeffery

*

I open the door to a yardful of starlings
and one crow   on the roof

angie werren

*

braking
for a rain-sleek
       fox

Mark Holloway

*

all it takes
is the right height
to see the curve
from sea to sea

June O'Reilly

Am Volkspark
An elderly lady with alpine walking sticks and a body that resembles them, threads her way through the park. She has fire in her eyes and an enormous, grey fur hat on her head.

Kate Brown

*

The scar is old, half-an-inch wide, and runs from earlobe
                                      to mouth corner,
smooth slash between dark stubble. *The Encyclopedia of*
                                      Things That Never Were
lays open on his lap; he is drunk, too close and wants
                                      conversation.
I fixed stare out the bowel-train window, 'Alight here
                                      for Tenement House'.

JoAnne Mackay

*

Lake ice,
window of the
water house below.

Hold a piece up
in front of the sun
it becomes my window too.

Mary Dusing

Feet on the back stairs.
Morning gamelan.

Annie Kerr

*

fingers, winter dry
catch laundry, the smooth sheet
the cleansed shirts

the day is cold but bright
we hang sheets to catch sun
my daughter laughing
at the cloth over her head

how each thing steams
how we catch ourselves
watching our breath
how the inside becomes outside

Lara Payne

*

and the seagulls took
the sun under their
wings

Linda Framke

Padmasana
sitting in lotus pose
holding the world in my palms
a yellow leaf
spirals past me
while the dog farts

Britta Froehling

*

Solar collector—the cat stretches her full-length on the couch, catching the noonday sun, moving as the sun moves.

Nancy Brady

*

Cormorant:
Sickle-necked. Reptilian.
Regards me with unblinking eye.

Julie Singleton

*

scornful crows
scurry after me
like clacking castanets

Sidney Bending

With the wane of the day
dissolving into evening primrose
the slightest bit of nothing
creeps up on me

Julie Gengo

*

5:30 a.m
Beyond our yard and his
I see my neighbor's window –
a square of light in the dark.

Kelly Eastlund

*

gray day
I paint my lips red
and kiss the sky!

Terri L. French

*

I realized
    pomegranates are best eaten
naked.

Melissa Richardson

ice at the lake-edge
the toddler's
red boot

Joanna M. Weston

*

Sleep:
At sunset, a hundred
sparrows
tiny
swoosh down in a gulp of brown feathers
hide behind the flood of fresh
frangipani blossoms.

Chryselle D'Silva Dias

*

Just the smell of coffee is enough
Just a glimpse of the moon is enough

Olivia Dresher

*

Blue dusk,
stars slowly puncturing the sky.

Lori Ann Bloomfield

How vulnerable we are

At first, writing small stones, I still felt the pressure of producing. Odd how vulnerable we are, but then turning over these small stones is turning over parts of our...selves and then showing others. Even when we keep ourselves out of the observation, the observation still comes from some part of our thoughts. We may be writers recording, we may, or may not set up a speaker as a buffer, but each word, each grain of every stone, comes from a part of our minds, our hearts, our souls. And then we set the stones on a path, or atop a wall, or on a window sill, for others to spot and pick up, and, if they like what they see, to place the stones in their pockets to carry home.

Because of the sense of community and the support, the vulnerability disappeared at some point in the process. And to continue the support, the writers' community * you have formed is a safe place to be ourselves, to not hide, or worry about what we write and whether it is ready, or not, for others' eyes.

~Margo Roby, *small stone* writer

* *http://writingourwayhome.ning.com*

What is a *small stone*?

A *small stone* is a short piece of writing that precisely captures a fully-engaged moment.

Small stones don't conform to a strict form, like haikus or sonnets. *Small stones* can be written in verse or in sentences, in plain or poetic language. They can be three words long or one hundred words long. They usually describe a single careful observation, and they usually focus on 'the other' rather than the writer. Polished *stones* will sound good and look good on the page, as well as conjuring something fresh in the mind of the reader.

The process of finding *small stones* is as important as the finished product. To become ready to receive a *small stone*, we need to become still. We need to keep our eyes (and ears, nose, mouth, fingers, feelings and mind) open.

History of *small stones*

In 2005, on a long rainy drive home from the seaside, I thought about my current blog with its long prose pieces and longed instead for somewhere more minimalist, somewhere more sacred. I wanted to create a place where I could really indulge my love of language, and where every word would count. All things begin with a name. I started playing around with labels for this new space.

The phrase 'a small stone' floated up from the ether. I dismissed it immediately. It was too plain, too ordinary. I wanted my blog to dazzle, to astonish, to be alive. A part of me wouldn't let it go. It took me on a long beach walk, where my eyes snagged on a smooth pale-blue oval stone. I bent to pick it up and put it in my pocket. I flipped it over, felt the weight of it in my hand, and brushed my fingertips over its granular surface.

I stopped looking for a snazzier blog title. Instead I decided to look for a small stone every day for a year. That was 2005, and I'm still going. In 2008 I started collecting other people's *small stones* at 'a handful of stones', and in 2011 we launched 'a river of stones' with the January write-a-small-stone-every-day challenge. The river shows no signs of abating.

Why should you write *small stones*?

It is difficult to pay attention. 'Life' (feeding the cats, paying the mortgage, taking out the rubbish) continually gets in the way, as do the thoughts we have about these tasks. "When will I have time?" "Why can't I have a more glamorous life?"

Writing a *small stone* requires us to let go of our busy thoughts for a few seconds and to become open to what is around us. It asks us to really notice the 'other' - without seeing it purely as a job-to-be-done or as a prop to our rapacious egos.

Some people conceptualise this 'other' as something sacred, and so writing *small stones* becomes a spiritual practice. Others use *small stones* to connect with the spirit of nature, with other people, and with themselves. Whatever you observe, you will be practising your capacity for clear-seeing, for opening yourself up.

One of the side-effects of writing *small stones* is that we begin to find it easier to love the 'other'. We don't have such an urgent need for it to be a particular way. We can understand it more, and so we can forgive it. We can notice its beauty, even in the midst of its ugliness.

Where will you find *small stones*?

Small stones are all around us. All you have to do is pause, become open, and let them appear. You'll know one when you see one, because it will set off a small burst of feeling or recognition inside you.

You might be struck by the streaks of pink clouds in the sky, or the particles of soot clinging to your fire-place. An overheard conversation might allude to something that feels true. Whatever you notice, it will have the quality of coming to you fresh, through clear eyes.

How do you pick up your *small stones*?

The best way is to catch *small stones* is as they occur in the wild, by waiting for them to appear. Carry a note-book around with you and jot down some notes straight away. If you don't have any paper, the back of your hand will do. If you don't have a pen, play around with some words in your head and hold on tight until you can catch them on paper.

You can also catch a *small stone* in retrospect, by writing down a moment from earlier in the day. What stood out for you? How accurately can you remember it? Finally, the least effective way (but infinitely better than not writing a *small stone* at all!) is to trawl back through your day and think about where you've been and what you've done. Are there any *small stones* lurking in the shadows?

Make your observation, and write it down. Describe what you can see, and what you can hear. Write down what it tastes like, what thoughts or feelings rise up in you. Tell us exactly what your dog's fur feels like as it slides against your palms. Show us your world, and let us inhabit it.

To begin with, write down a lot. Describe everything in great detail. Let your imagination off its leash. When you've written down everything you can think of, go through what you've got and choose the words (as few as you can) that point you towards the essence of what you originally noticed. There - a *small stone*!

How do you polish up your *small stones*?

Polishing your *small stones* will help you to learn more about what you've seen. It will also result in a piece of writing that sounds better in your mouth and looks better on the page. One of the joys of being a writer is producing something inherently beautiful – this can be immensely satisfying (and it can also be unbelievably frustrating when the writing isn't going so well!)

The following check-list will help you to polish your *small stone* up until it is as perfect as you can make it.

- ❖ **Have you used precise language?** Was the berry red or was it scarlet? Is the water leaking or seeping? If in doubt, get out a thesaurus.

❖ **Is every single word necessary?** In a short piece of writing, every word must earn its keep. If it doesn't add anything, take it out.

❖ **Have you shown us something or told us something?** Show, don't tell. It is usually more effective to describe something and let the reader draw their own conclusions, than to 'spell it out'. Rather than writing 'the sky was beautiful', show us the sky. What colour is it? What texture?

❖ **How does it look on the page?** Do you want to use a title? How do you want to use capital letters and punctuation? Do you want to break up your sentence into shorter pieces and put them underneath each other? Fiddle about with the words on the page until they look right.

❖ **How does it sound when you read it out loud?** Do you stumble over a particular phrase? What are the rhythms like? The alliterations and assonances? Could you use an alternative different word for 'shining' which would sound better with the other words in the piece?

❖ **How original is it?** Have you looked at something ordinary in a fresh way? It's more difficult to be original about blackbirds and sunsets than it is about the mud on your shoes or the sound of stirring your tea.

❖ **How much of 'you' is in it?** If you've spent a long time telling us how you feel about what you've observed, or what conclusions we can draw from what you noticed, then it's not likely to be a pure observation of 'the other'. Edit these bits out and see how you feel about what's left.

There are no right or wrong answers to any of these questions. As a writer, you will discover your own unique 'way with words'. The important thing is that you take the time to consider them. Enjoy your polishing – try to find a spirit of play.

What can you do with your *small stones*?

A lot of people write their *small stones* into a beautiful notebook and leave them there. Others share them with the world on their blogs, over coffee with their friends, on the 'Writing Our Way Home' forum (http://writingourwayhome.ning.com), on Twitter, at poetry readings, or on Facebook.

Connecting with other *small stone* writers

There is a whole community of writers out there (many of them in this book) who are interested in using writing as a way of connecting with the world. They don't just write *small stones* – they read other people's *small stones* and post encouraging comments, they discuss what kind of attention we use when we search for *small stones*, they keep each other going when the going gets tough.

The best place to connect with these people is at the 'Writing Our Way Home' community forum, at www.writingourwayhome.com. Here you can post your daily *small stone*, get advice and encouragement on how to write daily, meet like-minded writers and much more. It's free to join – we hope to see you there.

The river of stones blog has news of our current projects, including our regular write-a-*small-stone*-a-day challenge months – it's at www.ariverofstones.blogspot.com. There is also a blogzine where you can submit your *small stones* - www.ahandfulofstones.com.

We have a page on Facebook, and people tweet their *small stones* using the #aros hashtag.

There is more information about all these links and more (including a free e-book about writing *small stones*) at our main site – www.writingourwayhome.com.

Do join us!

Slim Eating

Guilt-Free Desserts

All Rights Reserved. No part of this publication may be reproduced in any form or by any means, including scanning, photocopying, or otherwise without prior written permission of the copyright holder. Copyright ©
2014

Introduction

Eating clean – an intriguing yet somewhat esoteric concept. What is it exactly? Well, we know that our bodies were not designed to eat fast food, sugar and processed junk. These unnatural foods are toxic to us and cause disease, weight gain and cancer.

Mother Nature provides us with everything we need to eat in order to live a healthy, long life. This does not mean you should eat a boring diet made up of grilled meat and lettuce every day. The good news is that you can still enjoy your favourite desserts while eating slim. You just have to know *how* to do it. This book provides 30 ideas for mind-blowing desserts that are so delicious that nobody will even notice they are healthy. Go ahead – you can feel great about serving these desserts to your loved ones!

Table of Contents

Skinny Apple Crumble

Creamy Pumpkin Cheesecake

Gingerbread Cookies

Basic Banana Bread

Scrumptious Cinnamon Buns

Yummy Strawberry Rhubarb Pie

Sweet Raisin Pecan Cake

Slim Cranberry Almond Cookies

Pineapple Coconut Cake

Mocha Brownie Bites

Cinnamon Raisin Bread

Easy Poppy Seed Muffins

Blackberry Dumplings

Skinny Coconut Baked Donut

Delicious Apple Pastries

Healthy Lemon Coconut Bars

Chocolate Pecan Shortbread Cookies

Red Velvet Bars
Wild Mince Meat Pie
Baked Peaches
Tiramisu
Chocolate Almond Biscotti
Ginger Mango Sherbet
Pineapple Upside Down Cake
Cashew Chocolate Mousse
Sweet Cinnamon Pretzel
Healthy Refrigerator Carrot Cake
Ginger Punch Pudding
Quick Tropical Sorbet

Skinny Apple Crumble

Prep Time: 20 minutes

Cook Time: 50 minutes

Servings: 8

INGREDIENTS

Crust

2 cups almond flour

1 cage-free egg

2 tablespoons coconut oil (or cacao butter or ghee)

1/4 teaspoon Celtic sea salt

Filling

5 apples

1/2 cup date butter (or raw honey or agave)

1/2 lemon

1 teaspoon ground cinnamon

1/2 teaspoon vanilla

1/4 teaspoon ground nutmeg

1/4 teaspoon Celtic sea salt

Topping

1/2 cup almond flour

1/2 cup pecans

1/2 cup shredded coconut

1/4 cup cold cacao butter (or coconut butter, ghee or coconut oil)

1/4 cup raw honey (or agave)

1/4 cup dried pitted dates

2 tablespoons ground flax

1 teaspoon cinnamon

INSTRUCTIONS
1. Preheat oven to 375 degrees F.
2. For *Crust*, blend almond flour and salt in small mixing bowl. Add egg and oil or butter. Mix until dough forms. Press into pie pan or baking dish with hand or wooden spoon. Set aside.
3. For *Filling*, core and peel apples. Cut into thin slices and add to large mixing bowl. Add sweetener, salt and spices. Juice 1/2 lemon over apples and mix to combine. Press apples firmly into *Crust*.
4. For *Topping*, add dates and honey or agave to food processor or high-speed blender. Process until coarsely ground, about 1 minute. Add butter or oil, almond flour, pecans, coconut, flax and cinnamon. Pulse until finely chopped or coarsely ground. Sprinkle *Topping* over apples.
5. Bake 40 - 50 minutes, until apples are cooked and *Topping* is browned and crisp.
6. Remove from oven and allow to cool at least 5 minutes.
7. Slice and serve warm. Or let cool completed and serve room temperature.

Creamy Pumpkin Cheesecake

Prep Time: 15 minutes*
Cook Time: 10 Minutes
Servings: 12

INGREDIENTS

Crust

1/2 cup coconut flour

1/4 cup cacao butter (or coconut butter or coconut oil)

1/4 cup raw honey (or agave or date butter)

1/2 cup shredded or flaked coconut

Filling

1 1/2 cups raw cashews

1 cup organic pumpkin purée

1/2 cup date butter (or agave or raw honey)

1/2 cup full-fat coconut milk

1/2 cup coconut oil (or cacao or coconut butter, melted)

1 lemon

1 1/2 teaspoons vanilla

2 teaspoons ground cinnamon

1/2 teaspoon ground nutmeg

1/4 teaspoon ground clove

1/4 teaspoon ground ginger

1/2 teaspoon Celtic sea salt

Water

INSTRUCTIONS
1. *For *Filling*, soak cashews in enough water to cover for at least 4 hours to overnight in refrigerator. Drain and rinse.
2. Preheat oven to 375 degrees F.
3. For *Crust*, place all ingredients in food processor or high-speed blender. Process until well ground and mixture sticks together, about 2 minutes.
4. Press *Crust* firmly into bottom of spring form pan with hands. Bake about 8 minutes, then set aside.
5. For *Filling*, zest *then* juice lemon into clean food processor or high-speed blender. Add soaked cashews, pumpkin purée, sweetener, coconut milk, oil or butter, vanilla, salt and spices. Process until smooth, about 2 - 3 minutes.
6. Pour *Filling* into *Crust* and smooth with spatula.
7. *Cover pie with parchment, if preferred, and set aside in refrigerator at least 4 hours to set.
8. Slice and serve chilled.

Gingerbread Cookies

Prep Time: 5 minutes

Cook Time: 15 minutes

Servings: 12

INGREDIENTS

1 cup almond flour

2 cage-free eggs

1/2 cup dried pitted dates

1/4 cup raw honey (or dark agave)

1/4 cup coconut oil (or cacao butter, melted)

1/2 teaspoon baking soda

1/2 teaspoon baking powder

2 teaspoons ground ginger

1 teaspoon ground cinnamon

1 teaspoon vanilla

1/2 teaspoon ground cloves

1/2 teaspoon ground black pepper

1/4 teaspoon Celtic sea salt

Natural sarsaparilla or root beer beverage, or nut milk (optional)

INSTRUCTIONS

1. Preheat oven to 350 degrees F. Line sheet pan with parchment or baking mat.

2. Add dates, honey or agave and eggs to food processor or high-speed blender. Process until thick smooth mixture forms, about 2 minutes.
3. Add almond flour, oil or butter, baking soda and powder, salt and spices to processor. Process until thick mixture comes together, about 1 minute. Add sarsaparilla, root beer or nut milk to thin as necessary. Batter should resemble thick cookie dough.
4. From rounds and place on prepares sheet pan. Flatten into disks.
5. Bake 10 - 15 minutes, until browned around edges and cooked through, but still soft.
6. Remove from oven and let cool at about 10 minutes.
7. Transfer to serving dish and serve warm. Or cool completely and serve room temperature.

Basic Banana Bread

Prep Time: 5 minutes
Cook Time: 40 minutes
Servings: 8

INGREDIENTS

1 cup almond flour

1/4 cup coconut flour

2 overripe bananas

2 cage-free eggs

1/4 cup raw honey (or agave, date butter or stevia)

1/4 cup coconut oil (or coconut or cacao butter, melted) (or unsweetened applesauce or nut butter)

1 tablespoon baking powder

2 teaspoons ground cinnamon

1/2 teaspoon ground nutmeg

1 teaspoon vanilla

1/2 teaspoon Celtic sea salt

INSTRUCTIONS

1. Preheat oven to 350 degrees F. Coat small or medium loaf pan with coconut oil.
2. Peel bananas and add to medium mixing bowl. Beat with hand mixer or whisk. Add eggs, oil or butter, and sweetener. Beat well, about 1 - 2 minutes.

3. In separate bowl, blend flours, baking powder, salt and spices. Pour banana mixture into flour mixture and stir to combine.
4. Pour batter into prepared loaf pan and bake for 30 - 40 minutes, or until browned and firm in the center.
5. Remove from oven and set aside to cool.
6. Slice and serve warm. Or allow to cool completely and serve room temperature.

Scrumptious Cinnamon Buns

Prep Time: 15 minutes

Cook Time: 30 minutes

Servings: 8

INGREDIENTS

Rolls

3 cups almond flour

3 cage-free eggs

1/2 cup date butter (or raw honey or agave)

1/4 cup ground chia seed (or flax meal)

1/4 cup tapioca flour (or arrowroot powder)

1/4 cup nut milk

2 teaspoons baking powder

1/4 teaspoon Celtic sea salt

Coconut oil (for cooking)

Filling

1/4 cup ghee (or cacao or coconut butter, melted)

3/4 cup dried pitted dates

2 tablespoons ground cinnamon

Icing

1/2 cup raw honey (or date butter or agave)

1/2 cup full-fat coconut milk

INSTRUCTIONS
1. Preheat oven to 350 degrees F. Line cake pan or round baking dish with coconut oil. Cover cutting board with parchment and coat heavily with coconut oil.
2. For *Rolls*, heat nut milk in small pan over medium heat. Whisk in tapioca until combined. Remove from heat.
3. Add eggs to food processor or high-speed blender. Process until pale and silky, about 2 minutes. Add sweetener, chia meal, baking powder and salt. Process until combined, about 1 minute.
4. Add egg mixture and tapioca mixture to medium mixing bowl. Beat in almond flour 1 cup at a time with hand mixer or whisk.
5. Place dough on prepared parchment. Oil hands to prevent sticking and press dough into large 1/2 inch thick rectangle.
6. For *Filling*, add ghee or butter, dates and cinnamon to clean food processor or high-speed blender. Process until finely ground or smooth, about 1 - 2 minutes.
7. Sprinkle *Filling* over dough. Roll dough into log along short edge using parchment paper. Use sharp knife or floss to slice log into rolls.
8. Place *Rolls* in prepared cake pan or baking dish. Bake about 15 minutes.
9. For *Icing*, add sweetener and coconut milk to clean food processor or high-speed blender. Process until well combined, about 1 minute.
10. Remove *Rolls* from oven and carefully pour Icing over *Rolls*. Place back in oven and bake 10 - 15 minutes, until *Rolls* are cooked through and *Icing* is warm.

11. Remove from oven and serve hot. Or let cool about 5 minutes and serve room warm.

Yummy Strawberry Rhubarb Pie

Prep Time: 10 minutes

Cook Time: 50 minutes

Servings: 12

INGREDIENTS

Crust

2 cups almond flour

1 cage-free egg

2 tablespoons coconut oil (or cacao butter or ghee)

1/4 teaspoon Celtic sea salt

Filling

1/4 cup tapioca flour (or arrowroot powder)

2 1/2 cups diced rhubarb (fresh or frozen)

2 1/2 cups fresh strawberries (sliced)

3/4 cup raw honey (or agave or date butter)

1/2 lemon

1 teaspoon ground cinnamon

1 teaspoon vanilla

INSTRUCTIONS

1. Preheat oven to 350 degrees F.
2. For *Crust*, blend almond flour and salt in small mixing bowl. Add egg and oil or butter. Mix until dough forms. Press into pie pan with hand or wooden spoon.

3. Bake *Crust* about 10 minutes.
4. For *Filling*, add strawberries and rhubarb to medium pot. Heat over medium-high heat and stir lightly. Zest *then* juice lemon into pot. Cook about 5 minutes to release juices.
5. Sift tapioca over fruit and stir to combine. Cook about 5 minutes, then add sweetener, vanilla and cinnamon. Remove from heat.
6. Remove *Crust* from oven and carefully pour in *Filling*.
7. Bake about 35 - 40 minutes, or until fruit is set.
8. Remove from oven and let cool about 20 minutes.
9. Slice and serve warm. Or let cool completely and serve room temperature.

Sweet Raisin Pecan Cake

Prep Time: 10 minutes

Cook Time: 40 minutes

Servings: 12

INGREDIENTS

6 cage-free eggs

1 cup coconut flour

1/2 cup date butter (or agave or raw honey)

1/2 cup unsweetened applesauce

1/2 cup nut milk

1/4 cup coconut oil (or cacao or coconut butter, melted)

1 cup pecans

1/2 cup raisins

1 teaspoon vanilla

1 teaspoon baking soda

1 teaspoon baking powder

1/2 teaspoon Celtic sea salt

INSTRUCTIONS

1. Preheat oven to 350 degrees F. Coat Bundt pan with coconut oil.
2. Add egg whites to food processor or high-speed blender. Process until light and frothy, about 1 - 2 minutes.
3. Add egg yolks, coconut flour, sweetener, applesauce, nut milk, oil or butter, baking soda and powder, vanilla and salt. Process until

well combined batter comes together, about 2 minutes. Chop pecans and stir in with raisins.
4. Pour batter into prepared Bundt pan and bake for about 40 minutes, until golden brown and toothpick inserted halfway between edge and center of pan comes out clean.
5. Remove from oven and allow to cool at least 10 minutes.
6. Place serving dish over pan, invert and release cake to plate.
7. Slice and serve warm. Or let cool completely and serve room temperature.

Slim Cranberry Almond Cookies

Time: 10 minutes

Cook Time: 15 minutes

Servings: 12

INGREDIENTS

1 1/2 cups almond flour

1 cage-free egg

1/4 cup coconut oil (or cacao or coconut butter)

1/4 cup raw honey (or agave or date butter)

1/4 cup almond butter

1/4 cup almonds

1/4 cup dried cranberries

1/2 teaspoon baking powder

1 teaspoon vanilla

1/4 teaspoon Celtic sea salt

INSTRUCTIONS
1. Preheat oven to 350 degrees F. Line sheet pan with parchment or baking mat.
2. Sift flour, baking powder and salt into medium mixing bowl. Beat with whisk or hand mixer to lighten. Add egg, oil or butter, sweetener, almond butter, vanilla and salt. Mix well to form dough.
3. Chop almonds and add to bowl with cranberries. Mix to combine.

4. Shape dough into 12 balls and place on prepared baking sheet. Flatten slightly with hand or spatula.
5. Place in oven and bake 10 - 15 minutes, until golden brown along edges.
6. Remove from oven and let cool 5 minutes.
7. Serve warm. Or transfer to wire rack to cool completely and serve room temperature.

Pineapple Coconut Cake

Prep Time: 10 minutes

Cook Time: 45 minutes

Servings: 12

INGREDIENTS

6 cage-free eggs

3/4 cup coconut flour

1 cup flaked coconut

1 1/2 cups pineapple (diced)

1/2 cup raw honey (or agave or date butter)

1/2 cup coconut oil (or cacao or coconut butter, melted)

1 teaspoon baking soda

1 teaspoon baking powder

1 teaspoon vanilla

1/2 teaspoon Celtic sea salt

INSTRUCTIONS

1. Preheat oven to 350 degrees F. Lightly coat square or rectangular baking dish with coconut oil.
2. Add eggs to food processor or high-speed blender. Process until pale and lightened, about 2 minutes.
3. Add flour, coconut, pineapple, sweetener, oil or butter, baking soda, baking powder, vanilla and salt. Process until well combined, about 1 - 2 minutes.

4. Pour batter into prepared baking dish and bake about 45 minutes, until golden brown and firm in the center.
5. Remove from oven and allow to cool about 10 minutes.
6. Slice and serve warm. Or let cool completely and serve room temperature.

Mocha Brownie Bites

Prep Time: 5 minutes

Cook Time: 25 minutes

Servings: 16

INGREDIENTS

4 cage-free eggs

1 cup cocoa powder

1/4 cup coconut oil

1/4 cup full-fat coconut milk

1/4 cup sweetener*

2 teaspoons instant espresso (or instant coffee)

1 teaspoon vanilla

INSTRUCTIONS

1. Preheat oven to 350 degrees F. Lightly oil square baking dish or line with parchment.
2. Add eggs, coconut oil, coconut milk and sweetener to medium mixing bowl and beat with hand mixer or whisk. Sift in cocoa powder, espresso and vanilla. Beat until well combined.
3. Pour batter into prepared baking pan and bake for 20 - 25 minutes, until set.
4. Allow to cool completely.
5. Slice and serve room temperature. Or refrigerate and serve chilled.

raw honey, agave nectar or maple syrup

Cinnamon Raisin Bread

Prep Time: 5 minutes
Cook Time: 20 minutes
Servings: 12

INGREDIENTS

3/4 cup coconut flour
3/4 cup almond flour
1/4 cup ground chia seed (or flax meal)
2 cage-free eggs
1/2 cup raisins
1/2 cup coconut oil
1/2 cup unsweetened applesauce
1/4 cup sweetener*
2 tablespoons ground cinnamon
1 teaspoon baking powder
1 teaspoon sea salt
1/2 teaspoon ground black pepper (optional)

INSTRUCTIONS

1. Preheat oven to 350 degrees F. Line baking pan with parchment or coat with coconut oil.
2. In large bowl, whisk eggs with hand mixer or whisk until frothy and light. Add coconut oil, sweetener and applesauce. Blend until combined.

3. Sift coconut and almond flour, chia meal, baking powder, salt and spices into wet ingredients. Beat until smooth and well combined. Stir in raisins.
4. Pour batter into prepared baking pan.
5. Bake for 20 - 25 minutes, or until golden brown and firm to the touch.
6. Remove from oven and let cool about 5 minutes.
7. Slice and serve warm. Or allow to cool completely and serve room temperature.

NOTE: Bake in oiled loaf pan for 40 - 45 minutes for **Cinnamon Raisin Bread** loaf.

stevia, raw honey or agave nectar

Easy Poppy Seed Muffins

Prep Time: 5 minutes
Cook Time: 20 minutes
Servings: 12

INGREDIENTS

6 eggs
1/2 cup coconut flour
1/4 cup coconut oil
1/4 cup sweetener*
1 teaspoon vanilla
1 teaspoon poppy seeds
1/2 teaspoon baking soda
Juice of 2 lemons
Zest of 2 lemons

INSTRUCTIONS

1. Preheat oven to 350 degrees F. Oil muffin pan or line with paper liners.
2. Zest, *then* juice 2 lemons. Add to large mixing bowl with eggs, coconut oil, sweetener and vanilla. Beat with hand mixer or whisk until well combined.
3. Sift coconut flour and baking soda into wet ingredients, and mix until smooth. Stir in poppy seeds.
4. Use ice cream scoop or tablespoon to pour batter into prepared muffin pan.

5. Place in oven and bake for about 20 minutes, or until golden around edges and toothpick inserted into middle comes out clean.
6. Remove from oven and let cool for 5 minutes.
7. Serve warm. Or allow to cool completely and serve room temperature.

raw honey or agave nectar

Blackberry Dumplings

Prep Time: 15 minutes

Cook Time: 20 minutes

Servings: 8

INGREDIENTS

Blackberry Filling

2 1/2 cups blackberries (fresh or frozen)

2 - 4 tablespoons sweetener*

2 tablespoons tapioca flour

1/2 teaspoon ground black pepper

Zest of 1/2 lemon

Dumplings

1/4 cup coconut flour

3/4 cup almond flour

3 tablespoons cold coconut oil

1 teaspoon baking powder

1/2 teaspoon ground cinnamon

1/4 teaspoon sea salt

2 cage-free eggs

2 tablespoon sweetener

1 teaspoon vanilla

Zest of 1/2 lemon

INSTRUCTIONS

1. For *Dumplings*, sift coconut flour, almond flour, baking powder and salt into small mixing bowl. Cut in cold coconut oil with fork until crumbly. Place in freezer for 10 minutes.
2. Preheat oven to 400 degrees F.
3. For *Blackberry Filling*, add blackberries, sweetener, black pepper and lemon zest to medium pot. Heat over medium heat and bring to simmer. Whisk in tapioca flour and simmer about 10 minutes.
4. Pour hot blackberries into casserole dish and place in hot oven.
5. In medium bowl, beat eggs, sweetener, lemon zest, cinnamon and vanilla. Add chilled flour mixture to eggs and mix until dough comes together.
6. Carefully remove dish from oven and drop 8 dumplings onto bubbling berries.
7. Return dish to oven and bake 15 - 20 min, until dumplings are golden, set and cooked through.
8. Remove dish from oven and allow to cool about 5 minutes.
9. Serve warm. Or allow to cool completely and serve room temperature.

stevia, raw honey or agave nectar

Skinny Coconut Baked Donut

Prep Time: 5 minutes

Cook Time: 20 minutes

Servings: 6

INGREDIENTS

Donuts

1 3/4 cups almond flour

1 tablespoon coconut flour

2 eggs

1/3 cup coconut oil

1/4 cup unsweetened applesauce

1/4 cup sweetener*

2 tablespoons nut milk

2 teaspoons vanilla

3/4 teaspoon baking soda

1/2 teaspoon sea salt

Topping

1/2 cup flaked or shredded coconut

1/4 cup full-fat coconut milk

2 tablespoon sweetener

1/4 teaspoon vanilla

INSTRUCTIONS

1. Preheat oven to 350 degreesF. Lightly coat donut pan with coconut oil.
2. Add almond and coconut flours, baking soda and salt to food processor or high-speed blender. Process for 1 minute.
3. Add eggs, sweetener, coconut oil, applesauce, nut milk and vanilla. Process until light, thick batter forms, about 1 - 2 minutes.
4. Pour batter into donut pan until wells are 3/4 full.
5. Place in oven and bake for about 20 minutes, until dough is set and lightly browned.
6. For *Topping*, combine coconut milk, sweetener and vanilla in small mixing bowl.
7. Remove pan from oven at let cool about 5 minutes. Then remove donuts from pan.
8. Dip donuts in coconut icing then sprinkle with flaked or shredded coconut.
9. Transfer decorated donuts to serving dish.
10. Serve warm. Or let cool completely and serve room temperature.

NOTE: Bake in 8 mini cake pans or specialty cake pop pans lightly coated with coconut oil for fillable donuts or donut holes if you do not have a donut pan.

stevia, raw honey or agave nectar

Delicious Apple Pastries

Prep Time: 20 minutes

Cook Time: 20 minutes

Servings: 4

INGREDIENTS

Crust

2 cups almond flour

2 cage-free eggs

3 tablespoons coconut oil

1 tablespoon sweetener*

1/2 teaspoon baking soda

1/2 teaspoon baking powder

1 teaspoon ground cinnamon

1/4 teaspoon sea salt

Filling

2 sweet apples

1/4 cup water

1 teaspoon tapioca flour

1 tablespoon ground cinnamon

1/2 teaspoon ground nutmeg

1 teaspoon vanilla

2 tablespoons sweetener * (optional)

2 tablespoons raisins (optional)

2 tablespoons chopped walnuts (optional)

DIRECTIONS

1. For *Crust*, sift almond flour into medium mixing bowl. Add baking soda and powder, cinnamon and salt.
2. Whisk eggs and sweetener in small mixing bowl, then add to flour mixture and combine. Slowly add coconut oil until malleable dough comes together.
3. Roll in plastic wrap or wrap tightly in parchment and refrigerate for 15 minutes.
4. Preheat oven to 400 degrees. Line sheet pan with parchment or baking mat. Cover cutting board with parchment. Heat medium pan over medium-high heat.
5. For *Filling*, peel and dice apples. Add apples to hot pan with water, tapioca, cinnamon, nutmeg, and sweetener and spices (optional).
6. Stir and simmer for about 5 - 8 minutes, until apples are tender and thick glaze forms. Remove from heat and add raisins and chopped walnuts (optional).
7. Remove dough from refrigerator. Roll dough out on parchment covered cutting board to about 1/8 inch thick square with rolling pin. Use sharp knife or pizza cutter to cut dough into 4 squares.
8. Scoop equal portions of *Filling* into center of one side of each dough square. Fold bare half of dough over filled half. Press edges together and secure seal, letting any trapped air escape. Repeat with remaining dough.
9. Arrange pies on lined sheet pan and bake 15 - 20 minutes, or until dough is golden and cooked through.
10. Serve immediately. Or allow to cool and serve room temperature.

stevia, raw honey or agave nectar

Healthy Lemon Coconut Bars

Prep Time: 15 minutes

Cook Time: 30 minutes

Servings: 12

INGREDIENTS

Crust

1/2 cup raw cashews

2/3 cup coconut flour

2 cage-free eggs

2 tablespoons coconut oil

2 tablespoons sweetener*

1 tablespoon flaked coconut

1 teaspoon fresh lemon juice

1/2 teaspoon baking soda

1/2 teaspoon vanilla

Filling

2 cage-free eggs

2 cage-free egg yolks

1 cup fresh lemon juice (about 6 lemons)

1/2 cup sweetener*

1/3 - 1/2 cup flaked coconut

2 tablespoons coconut flour

1 teaspoon lemon zest

INSTRUCTIONS

1. Preheat oven to 350 degrees F. Lightly coat rectangular baking dish with coconut oil, or line with parchment.
2. For *Crust*, add cashews and coconut to food processor or bullet blender and process until finely ground. Add remaining *Crust* ingredients to food processor and pulse until dough comes together.
3. Press dough into bottom of baking dish, and slightly up the sides. Dock crust with fork to prevent bubbling.
4. Place crust in oven and bake for 8 - 10 minutes.
5. For *Filling*, beat eggs, egg yolks, lemon juice, lemon zest and sweetener with hand mixer or whisk in medium bowl.
6. Sift in coconut flour and beat to combine. Let mixture sit for 5 minutes. Add flaked coconut and beat again to combine.
7. Pour *Filling* over par baked crust. Place in oven and bake 20 minutes, until center is set but still slightly jiggly.
8. Remove from oven and let cool for 20 minutes. Refrigerate about 20 minutes, until fully set and chilled.
9. Serve chilled or room temperature.

raw honey or agave nectar

Cocoa Spice Pinwheel Cookies

Prep Time: 10 minutes

Cook Time: 20 minutes

Servings: 12

INGREDIENTS

2 cups almond flour

2 tablespoon sweetener*

1 egg

1 teaspoon vanilla

1/2 teaspoon baking powder

1/4 teaspoon sea salt

Filling

2 tablespoons cocoa powder

2 tablespoons sweetener*

2 teaspoons ground cinnamon

1 teaspoon ground black pepper

1/2 teaspoon vanilla

INSTRUCTIONS

1. Preheat oven to 300 degrees F. Line sheet pan with parchment or baking mat. Prepare 2 additional sheets of parchment.
2. Add flour, egg, sweetener, vanilla, baking powder and salt to medium bowl. Blend with wooden spoon, then knead with hand to form thick dough.

3. Divide dough in half. Place half of dough in small mixing bowl. Add all *Filling* ingredients to bowl and mix until well combined.
4. Roll out each half of dough separately on parchment sheets. Roll into equal rectangles.
5. Place *Filling* rectangle on top of plain dough. Use parchment to help roll dough tightly along long edge into log.
6. Use sharp knife to cut log into 1/4 round slices. Place cookies on prepared sheet pan and bake about 10 minutes, until edges are golden brown.
7. Remove from oven and let cool about 5 minutes.
8. Serve warm. Or let cool completely and serve room temperature.

raw honey, agave nectar or maple syrup

Chocolate Pecan Shortbread Cookies

Prep Time: 5 minutes

Cook Time: 20 minutes

Servings: 12

INGREDIENTS

1 1/2 cups almond flour

1 1/2 cup pecans

1/4 cup cocoa powder

1/4 cup coconut oil (or melted cacao butter)

1/4 cup sweetener*

1 teaspoons vanilla

1/4 teaspoon baking soda

1/2 teaspoon sea salt

INSTRUCTIONS

1. Preheat oven to 300 degrees F. Line sheet pan with parchment or baking mat.
2. Add 1 cup pecans to food processor or high-speed blender and process until finely ground.
3. Add ground pecans to medium mixing bowl. Sift in almond flour, cocoa, baking soda and salt.
4. Chop remaining pecans and add to small mixing bowl. Add coconut oil or melted cacao butter, sweetener and vanilla to pecans. Mix to combine.
5. Pour wet mixture into dry ingredients and mix to form dough.

6. Use mini ice cream scoop or tablespoon to drop portions of dough onto prepared sheet pan.
7. Place in oven and bake 20 minutes, or until lightly browned.
8. Remove from oven and let cool at least 5 minutes.
9. Let cool completely and serve room temperature. Or serve warm.

raw honey, agave nectar or maple syrup

Red Velvet Bars

Prep Time: 20 minutes

Cook Time: 25 minutes

Servings: 16

INGREDIENTS

4 eggs

1/2 cup cocoa powder

1/2 cup almond flour

1/4 cup coconut oil

1/4 cup full-fat coconut milk

1/4 cup sweetener*

Juice of 1 beet

1 teaspoon vanilla

Topping

Coconut cream (settled from 1 can full-fat coconut milk)

2 - 4 tablespoons sweetener*

1/2 teaspoon vanilla

INSTRUCTIONS

1. Preheat oven to 350 degrees F. Lightly oil square baking dish or line with parchment.
2. Juice beet and add to medium mixing bowl. Add cocoa powder, eggs, coconut oil, coconut milk, sweetener and vanilla. Beat with hand mixer or whisk until well combined.

3. Pour batter into prepared baking pan and bake for 25 minutes, until set.
4. For *Topping*, beat coconut cream in medium mixing bowl until slightly thickened. Add sweetener and vanilla. Continue to beat until full thickened and fluffy, about 5 minutes.
5. Remove dish from oven and allow to cool. Frost with *Topping*.
6. Slice and serve room temperature. Or refrigerate and serve chilled.

* raw honey, agave nectar or maple syrup

Wild Mince Meat Pie

Prep Time: 20 minutes

Cook Time: 30 minutes

Servings: 8

INGREDIENTS

Crust

4 cups almond flour

2 eggs

1/4 cup coconut oil

1/2 teaspoon sea salt

Filling

12 oz grass-fed beef

2 sweet apples

2 tart apples

1 cup beef stock

1/4 cup sweetener*

Juice of 1 orange

Zest of 1 orange

1/4 cup arrowroot powder

1/4 cup apple cider vinegar

1 cup raisins

1/2 cup dried pitted dates

1/2 cup dried pitted prunes

1/2 cup dried cherries

2 teaspoons ground cinnamon

1 teaspoon ground nutmeg

1/2 teaspoon ground cloves

1/2 teaspoon ground black pepper

1/2 teaspoon salt

INSTRUCTIONS

1. Preheat oven to 350 degrees F. Heat large pot over medium-high heat and lightly coat with coconut oil. Lightly oil pie plate. Prepare 4 sheets of parchment.
2. Place beef in hot oiled pan and brown on each side for about 5 - 7 minutes, until just cooked through. Remove beef and set aside. Add beef stock to pot.
3. Mix all *Crust* ingredients together in medium bowl until dough forms. Divide dough in half and use rolling pin to roll dough between two parchment sheets into circles to fit about 1 inch over pie plate.
4. Press one dough circle into pie plate. Crimp edges to create small lip. Bake for 5 minutes, then remove and set aside.
5. Peel, core and grate or dice apples. Add to beef stock with sweetener, zest and juice of orange, vinegar, raisins, cherries, spices and salt. Dice beef, prunes and dates, and add to pot. Stir in arrowroot powder and thicken for a few minutes.
6. Once mixture comes together pour into par baked pie shell. Top with second dough sheet and crimp edges to fit into bottom crust.
7. Use sharp knife to slice top crust a few times for venting.
8. Bake pie for 30 minutes, or until crust is golden brown.
9. Remove from oven and allow to cool for about 20 minutes.

10. Slice and serve warm. Or allow to cool completely and serve room temperature.

stevia, raw honey or agave nectar

Baked Peaches

Prep Time: 5 minutes

Cook Time: 25 minutes

Servings: 4

INGREDIENTS

2 ripe peaches

1/4 cup walnuts

1/4 cup dried cranberries

2 tablespoons sweetener*

Juice of 1 orange

Zest of 1 orange

1 teaspoon cinnamon

1/2 teaspoon nutmeg

1/2 teaspoon ground allspice

INSTRUCTIONS

1. Preheat oven to 375 degrees F.
2. Slice peaches in half and remove pit. Place peach halves into glass or ceramic baking dish just big enough for them to fit snuggly.
3. Chop walnuts and toss with cranberries, sweetener, spices, juice and zest of orange in small bowl.
4. Fill peach halves with fruit and nut mixture. Pour excess liquid over peaches.
5. Bake in oven for about 20 - 25 minutes, until peaches are soften and lightly browned.

6. Remove from oven and let cool about 5 minutes.
7. Serve warm or room temperature.

stevia, raw honey or agave nectar

Tiramisu

Prep Time: 20 minutes*
Cook Time: 10 minutes
Servings: 8

INGREDIENTS

Lady Fingers

1/3 cup coconut flour
3 tablespoons arrowroot powder
4 eggs
1/4 cup sweetener**
1/2 teaspoon baking powder
1/2 teaspoon vanilla

2 tablespoons instant espresso (or instant coffee)
3/4 cup water
2 tablespoons cocoa powder

Cashew Mascarpone

2 cups cashews
2 tablespoons sweetener**
1 teaspoon lemon juice
1 teaspoon vanilla
Water

INSTRUCTIONS

1. *Soak 2 cups cashews in water overnight. Drain and rinse.
2. Preheat oven to 400 degrees F. Line two sheet pans with parchment paper. Fit pastry bag with 1/2 inch round tube, or cut 1/4 inch corner off sturdy kitchen storage bag (like Ziploc®).
3. Beat egg yolks, 1/4 cup sweetener and 1/2 teaspoon vanilla until thick and pale.
4. In separate bowl beat egg whites to stiff peaks with hand mixer or whisk in medium bowl. Fold half of egg whites into egg yolk mixture. Then sift in coconut flour, arrowroot powder and baking powder. Fold in remaining egg whites.
5. Scoop batter into pastry bag or storage bag. Place in tall wide contain and fold open end of bag over edge of container for greater ease.
6. Pipe 5 inch lady fingers onto parchment lined sheet pans about 2 inches apart. Bake for 8 minutes.
7. Remove cookies from oven and transfer full parchment sheet onto wire rack to cool completely. Do not try to remove warm cookies from parchment.
8. Process soaked cashews in food processor or bullet blender with sweetener, lemon juice, vanilla, and just enough water to smooth.
9. Bring 3/4 cup water just under a boil. Dissolve instant espresso or coffee in water and add to shallow dish.
10. Remove cooled lady fingers form parchment. Dip and roll each cookie in espresso, then arrange in single layer in glass baking dish. Cut cookies to fit into tight layer.

11. Dollop and spread on half of *Cashew Mascarpone*. Then add another layer of espresso dipped lady fingers. Top with last half of *Cashew Mascarpone* and sift on cocoa powder.
12. *Refrigerate at least 30 - 60 minutes.
13. Slice and serve chilled.

**stevia, raw honey or agave nectar*

Chocolate Almond Biscotti

Prep Time: 15 minutes

Cook Time: 35* minutes

Servings: 6

INGREDIENTS

1 cup almond flour

1/2 cup coconut flour

1/2 cup sweetener*

1/3 cup almonds

2 tablespoons cocoa powder

1 teaspoon vanilla

1/2 teaspoon baking soda

1/4 teaspoon sea salt

INSTRUCTIONS

1. Preheat oven to 350 degrees F. Line sheet pan with parchment paper. Heat medium pan over medium heat.
2. Add almonds to hot dry pan and toast for about 5 minutes, until aromatic. Stir frequently. Remove from heat and set aside.
3. In medium mixing bowl, blend almond flour, coconut flour, cocoa powder, baking soda and salt with hand mixer or whisk.
4. Beat in sweetener and vanilla until well combined and thick, sticky dough forms. Mix in toasted almonds with wooden spoon.
5. Form dough into flattened, uniform mound about 1 inch thick on sheet pan. Pat down mound to keep any almonds from sticking out.

6. Bake for about 15 minutes . Remove and allow to cool for about 15 minutes.
7. Use a very sharp serrated knife to carefully cut biscotti log into 1/2 - 2/3 inch slices. Hold onto the mound and cut on a diagonal. If it becomes crumbly, stick it back together.
8. Lace slice on sides and return to oven for 15 minutes.
9. Try to cut so that you're holding on to the edges of the log to keep it from crumbling. If parts come apart, you can stick them back together as the mixture is still kind of sticky.
10. Lay the biscotti flat and return to oven for 15 minutes.
11. *Turn oven off and leave oven door open a crack. Allow the biscotti to cool and dry for at least 2 hours.
12. Serve room temperature.

*raw honey, agave nectar, maple syrup, or any combination

Ginger Mango Sherbet

Prep Time: 5* minutes

Cook Time: 15 minutes

Servings: 4

INGREDIENTS

1 cup almond milk

1 cup coconut milk

2 ripe mangos

2 oz fresh ginger juice (about 8 inch bunch ginger root)

Juice of lime half

Zest of lime half

1 teaspoon vanilla

Bunch fresh mint

INSTRUCTIONS

1. *Freeze ice cream maker canister overnight before to make sure it is cold enough.
2. Add whole peeled ginger root to food processor. Or juice ginger and add to medium mixing bowl. Add mint leaves.
3. Slice, pit and peel mangos. Add to food processor or bullet blender with almond milk. Blend or process until smooth, then strain into medium mixing bowl.
4. Add coconut milk, juice and zest of half a lime, and vanilla. Mix well with whisk or hand mixer.

5. Turn on ice cream maker first, then carefully pour in mango mixture as ice cream maker paddle rotates.
6. Freeze for about 15 - 20 minutes. Then transfer frozen custard to serving dishes.
7. Serve immediately.

Pineapple Upside Down Cake

Prep Time: 15 minutes
Cook Time: 30 minutes
Servings: 12

INGREDIENTS

2 cups almond flour

8 - 12 slices organic canned pineapple in juice

8 - 12 pitted cherries

1/4 cup sweetener*

3 eggs

1/4 cup coconut oil

1/2 cup organic pineapple juice (reserved from can)

2 teaspoons baking soda

2 teaspoons vanilla

1/2 teaspoon sea salt

INSTRUCTIONS

1. Preheat oven to 350 degrees F. Line 9x13 baking dish with parchment paper, or coat with coconut oil.
2. Arrange pineapple slices and cherries on bottom of baking dish. Place in oven while you prepare the batter.
3. Beat egg whites to stiff peaks with hand mixer or whisk in medium mixing bowl. About 7 - 10 minutes.
4. In large mixing bowl, mix yolks, olive oil, sweetener, pineapple juice and vanilla.

5. Sift almond flour, baking soda and salt into yolk mixture. Beat until well combined.
6. Fold egg whites into batter until evenly combined.
7. Remove hot baking pan from oven, and spread light batter over pineapple and cherries. Smooth top with spatula.
8. Bake for 25 - 30 minutes, or until cake golden brown and firm but springy in the center. A toothpick inserted into the center should come out clean.
9. Remove pan from oven and allow to cool for 15 minutes. Turn cake out onto serving dish and remove parchment. Or scrape any stuck fruit from the pan and place back on cake.
10. Allow to cool another 15 minutes before serving. Serve room temperature or warm.

NOTE: For **Pineapple Upside Dow Cupcakes** , add a pineapple slice and cherry to muffin pan lined with paper liners or coated with coconut oil, then fill cups 2/3 full with batter and bake about 20 minutes.

stevia, raw honey or agave nectar

Cashew Chocolate Mousse

Prep Time: 5 minutes*

Servings: 2

INGREDIENTS

2 cups raw cashews

1/2 unsweetened flaked or shredded coconut

1/2 cup dried pitted dates

1/4 cup raw cacao powder

1 teaspoon vanilla

3 cups water

INSTRUCTIONS

1. *Soaked cashews and dates in 2 cups of water overnight. Separately soak coconut in 1 cup water overnight.
2. Add soaked coconut and water to high-speed blender. Process on high until smooth, about 1 minute.
3. Strain coconut mixture through nut milk bag or a few layers of cheese cloth. Squeeze out all excess liquid. Reserve coconut milk and set aside. Dry excess coconut, process until finely ground, and use as coconut flour.
4. Add drained soaked cashews and dates to clean food processor or high-speed blender with cacao powder and vanilla. Add 1/4 cup coconut milk and process on high until smooth and creamy. Add more coconut milk as necessary to reach desired consistency.

5. Pour mousse into serving dishes and serve immediately. Or freeze 15 minutes to thicken.
6. Serve room temperature or chilled.

Sweet Cinnamon Pretzel

Prep Time: 10 minutes

Cook Time: 20 minutes

Servings: 4

INGREDIENTS

Cinnamon Pretzel

1 cup coconut flour

1/2 cup tapioca flour/starch

1/2 cup coconut oil

1/2 cup water

2 dried dates

1 egg

2 tablespoon apple cider vinegar

1/2 teaspoon baking soda

1/2 teaspoon baking powder

2 teaspoons ground cinnamon

1/2 teaspoon vanilla

1/2 teaspoon ground ginger

1/2 teaspoon sea salt

Coconut Sweet Cream

1/4 cup full-fat coconut milk

2 tablespoons sweetener

1 tablespoon lemon juice

1/2 teaspoon vanilla

INSTRUCTIONS

1. Preheat oven to 350 degrees F. Heat medium pot over medium-high heat. Line sheet pan with parchment or baking mat.
2. Add dates, coconut oil, water, vinegar and salt to food processor or bullet blender and process until smooth. Pour mixture into pot. Bring to a boil and remove from heat.
3. Whisk in tapioca flour. Stir with wooden spoon or soft spatula until mixture gels and comes together.
4. Stir in baking soda and baking powder. Continue mixing for a minute. Mixture will foam and expand. Let mixture sit and cool about 5 minutes.
5. Sift in coconut flour and spices. Mix partially, then beat in egg. Mix until combined. Excess coconut flour may sit in bottom of bowl.
6. Turn out dough onto cutting board dusted with any excess coconut flour from mixture. Knead dough for 2 minutes.
7. Cut dough into 4 equal portions. Roll out pieces into ropes and twist to form classic pretzel twist. Pinch together any crumbled dough.
8. Arrange pretzels on lined sheet pan. Brush with coconut oil or full-fat coconut milk.
9. Place sheet pan in oven and bake about 25 minutes, until cooked through.
10. For *Coconut Sweet Cream*, mix coconut milk, vanilla, sweetener and lemon juice with had mixer or whisk until thick and creamy. Transfer to serving dish.

11. Serve pretzels immediately with *Coconut Sweet Cream*. Or allow pretzels to cool and refrigerate sweet cream, and serve chilled.

stevia, raw honey or agave nectar

Healthy Refrigerator Carrot Cake

Prep Time: 10 minutes*

Servings: 8

INGREDIENTS

Carrot Cake

2 - 3 large carrots

2 cups raw walnuts

1/2 cup raisins (or dried apricots)

1/2 cup flaked or shredded coconut

2 tablespoons raw pumpkin seeds

1/4 cup raw honey (or dried pitted dates)

1 teaspoon vanilla

1 teaspoon ground cinnamon

1/4 teaspoon ground nutmeg

1/4 teaspoon ground ginger (optional)

Cashew Cream Icing

1 cup raw cashews

1/2 large lemon

2 tablespoons raw honey (or dried pitted dates)

1 teaspoon vanilla

Water

INSTRUCTIONS

1. *For *Cashew Cream Icing*, separately soak cashews and dates (if using) in enough water to cover for 2 hours. Drain dates. Drain and rinse cashews.
2. For *Carrot Cake*, add carrots to food processor or high-speed blender and pulse to roughly chop. Add all *Carrot Cake* ingredients and process until coarsely ground but still slightly chunky, about 1 minute.
3. Transfer mixture to cake or baking pan and press firmly with hands.
4. For *Cashew Cream Icing*, juice lemon and add to clean food processor or high-speed blender with soaked cashews, soaked dates or honey, and vanilla. Process until smooth, about 2 minutes. Add enough date soaking liquid or water to reach desired consistency.
5. Spread *Cashew Cream Icing* over *Carrot Cake* and place in refrigerator at least 2 hours.
6. Slice and serve chilled. Or allow to warm slightly and serve.

Ginger Punch Pudding

Prep Time: 20 minutes*

Servings: 2

INGREDIENTS

1 young coconut (about 1 cup coconut meat and 1 cup coconut water)

2 - 4 tablespoons raw honey (or pitted dates)

1 1/2 inch piece fresh ginger

1/2 teaspoon ground ginger

1 teaspoon vanilla

Water (optional)

INSTRUCTIONS

1. * Soak dates in enough water to cover for at least 4 hours, or overnight in refrigerator (if using). Drain.
2. Remove flesh from fresh coconut and add to high-speed blender with 1 cup coconut water. Process until well blended and fairly smooth, about 1 - 2 minutes.
3. Peel ginger and grate into processor. Add vanilla, ground ginger, and honey or dates. Process until smooth, about 1 minute.
4. Transfer to serving dish and serve immediately or refrigerate at least 20 minutes and serve chilled.

Quick Tropical Sorbet

Prep Time: 30 minutes

Servings: 4

INGREDIENTS

2 coconuts (or 1 cup flaked coconut)

3 ripe mangos

1 orange

INSTRUCTIONS
1. *Freeze ice cream maker canister overnight.
2. *Soak flaked coconut in 2 cups water overnight in refrigerator, if using.
3. Add soaked coconut and soaking liquid to high-speed blender. Process until well blended and fairly smooth, about 1 - 2 minutes.
4. Or remove flesh from fresh coconuts and add to high-speed blender with 2 cups water. Process until well blended and fairly smooth, about 1 - 2 minutes.
5. Strain mixture through nut milk bag, cheesecloth or strainer back into blender.
6. Reserve pulp and set aside to dry and dehydrate, then use as coconut flour.
7. Cut mangos in half and remove peel. Roughly chop and add to blender. Zest *then* juice orange. Add to processor and process until smooth, about 1 minute.

8. Turn on ice cream maker. Slowly pour mixture into running ice cream maker. Let machine run until ice cream forms, about 20 minutes.
9. Transfer to serving dish and serve immediately. Or store in airtight container in freezer.

Printed in Great Britain
by Amazon